UNSTUCK AND UNSTOPPABLE

5 proven strategies to leverage your value, increase your visibility, and gain recognition to accelerate your career

Be Unstoppable

JEANNINE K BROWN

Jeannine

Gloria's Daughter Publishing Company, LLC

Unstuck and Unstoppable:
5 proven strategies to leverage your value, increase your visibility,
and gain recognition to accelerate your career

Jeannine K Brown

Published by Gloria's Daughter Publishing Company, LLC

Gloria's Daughter Publishing Company, LLC
E-mail: Contactus@unstuckandunstoppablebook.com

Limit of Liability/Disclaimer of Warranty:

Publishing and editorial team:
Author Bridge Media, www.AuthorBridgeMedia.com
Project Manager and Editorial Director: Helen Chang
Publishing Manager: Laurie Aranda

Library of Congress Control Number: 2021911293

ISBN: 978-1-7373281-0-0 -- paperback
978-1-7373281-9-3 -- ebook
978-1-7373281-8-6 – hardcover

Ordering Information:

Quantity sales. Special discounts are available on quantity purchases by
corporations, associations, and others. For details, contact the publisher
at the address above.

Printed in the United States of America

This book is dedicated to my mommy,
Gloria J. Brown.
You loved your career and inspired me
to seek the same love.
I miss you.

To my nieces Jazmyne Tiara and Sophia Grace and
nephew Evan Josiah, you are unstoppable.

CONTENTS

Acknowledgments.. vii

Introduction 1

Chapter 1   Overview... 9

Chapter 2   Make Boss Moves Now..........................21

Chapter 3   Be Strategic 41

Chapter 4   Leverage Your Impact, Communicate
Your Value... 63

Chapter 5   Master Negotiations 81

Chapter 6   Girl Power 98

Chapter 7   Be Daring.. 111

About the Author 121

ACKNOWLEDGMENTS

My bootstraps have been laced and tied by so many people because my accomplishments were not solo events. I acknowledge that I have never been alone—I live in an unstoppable community.

My grandparents, C. V. and Archie B. "Baby" Harrington, instilled in me a commitment to serve, a love for humanity, and the ability to make a vision come to life.

Dr. Percy J. Vaughn Jr., Dean (deceased), Lewis Easterly, Michael Wood, and Avery Munnings. Thank you for the doors you opened on my behalf to early opportunities and for demanding that I make boss moves.

Domanicka Dailey: since the day we met as interns in New York City, you've been the friend I need and the sister I wanted, and I'm grateful for your support and prayers.

Jamila Abston Mayfield: you told me that I have a gift to make people into great leaders, and now I've committed my life's work to this effort.

Crystal Martin: you asked me to speak about the glass ceiling, and *Unstuck and Unstoppable* was born.

Special thank you to Eboni Moss: I am grateful that you saw the vision and helped name this body of work.

Esther "Toni" Burt: you've stepped in as a bonus mother and cared for me as one of your own daughters, and I'm eternally grateful.

Thank you to my tribe: James E. Boone Jr., Justin and Desirae Butler, Mary Edwards, Herschel Frierson, Yolanda Hawkes, Jessica and Max Hill, Shantina Knox, Stephanie Mickens, Michael Mullins, Tim and Janie Nash, Michael Straughter, Renea Pierre, Royce Richardson, Leanard Rines, Uso and Nigel Sayers, Lorie Spratley, Elonia Taylor, Kathy White, Coretta Williams, and Daniel Worrell.

I hold the concerns and joys of my clients in my heart and my hands. I am grateful to be trusted by each person and company.

This book and my confidence to share my career and ideas were made possible because of the team at Author Bridge. Helen Chang: since the day we met, you have cheered me on and made me feel like an amazing thought leader.

INTRODUCTION

"Finally, I was able to see that if I had a contribution I wanted to make, I must do it, despite what others said. That I was okay the way I was. That it was alright to be strong."

—*Wangari Maathai*

Early in my career, I was often "the only ____" in the room. In many rooms, I was the only woman in a group of men. I was also the only Black person, the only person under thirty, and because my career started in the South, I was also the only person from the Midwest. For many years, I was no stranger to standing out in a crowded boardroom because of my differences. But I wanted to stand out for more than just being "the only." I had to find ways to be seen as more than just my gender and race.

But how?

I had to learn many things on my own. I quickly realized there was no course or training offered in school, or from my employers, on how to succeed at work. No one was going to diagram the steps to success, give me the secrets to overcome obstacles, or provide me with the formula for a happy career. I had to search for the unique qualities in my work product and my personality that made me stand out, the things that distinguished *me* from my peers. I had to take responsibility for my career and my success. I wanted to be seen, heard, and valued at work. In those first few years, I felt invisible. Invisible is a little dramatic, but I felt as if I was seen only for my visible differences.

Taking responsibility for my career success was an evolution that had many highs and a few lows. There were moments when I was stuck and did not know what to do next or how to handle a particular issue at work. I also experienced many unstoppable moments when everything aligned perfectly, and I was the boss chick who owned the room. No matter which season I was in, stuck or unstoppable, I knew it was up to me to learn and execute what it would take for me to be successful, and that I had to leave the door open for other women to rush through.

No one else would be responsible for my success.

The Confidence to Succeed

You do great work. You have the education, credentials, and the desire to succeed. But something keeps getting in the way of your career ambitions. Maybe you lack the confidence and self-awareness to communicate your professional value. You may not have the network or relationships you need to gain access to opportunities. Or you feel unclear about how best to perform at work, which leads to embarrassment.

You feel powerless.

Roadblocks are stalling your career acceleration, causing you to question whether it's the company, your manager . . . or you. You sit there and watch as the men around you climb the corporate ladder using relationship capital to gain access to opportunities that you didn't know existed. You ask yourself, where is the girls' club to help *you* get ahead? You can see the prize, but you need help: you don't know what you don't know.

It's no wonder that disappointment, frustration, and aggravation leave you feeling isolated and angry. The system is biased against you, and most days, it seems like no one is coming to help you navigate your career or increase your compensation. You wonder who's speaking up on your behalf about the value you add to the team.

There is this little voice in your head that tells you that this is as good as it gets. You tell yourself: do the work, get your paycheck, comply and assimilate, and maybe you'll get the promotion next year.

Some days it may seem like everybody has it together except you. Everyone seems so confident, and their careers are being fast-tracked. Corporate America isn't watching out for you—it doesn't reciprocate, it isn't loyal, and it doesn't have your back. Maybe corporate jobs aren't for you.

When we don't take action quickly enough, this is how it makes us feel. Stuck. Alone.

The truth is that it is up to you to control your career. You can make yourself so valuable—so indispensable—that they don't ever want to see you leave. You have to carve out space for yourself and get yourself unstuck.

It's Time to Ignite Your Career

Business moves at warp speed, with technological innovation driving constant change in every profession. You can't afford to wait until you master what you're currently doing, until you check all the boxes and "feel ready," before you strike out and demand a leadership role.

The time to go after what you want is now.

Though at times you feel utterly alone, the truth is that you stand in community, and there are so many others who want to see you rise—I want to see you rise and get what you want.

I am here with you, and I am going to share the strategies to success that I've gathered over my two-decade career in corporate leadership. You can use these techniques and lessons to take control of your career and feel empowered and equipped to take on the challenges in front of you.

There is no obstacle, no barrier, no situation that you can't overcome. You can leverage your value, increase your visibility, and gain the recognition you deserve to accelerate your career. You're here for a reason, you're perfectly suited, and you are unstoppable.

Get What You Want

Get the confidence to go through the process of negotiating a higher salary. Learn how to strategically develop a network that supports your career and be more influential in the workplace. Identify and go after the business opportunities that you want. Find supportive networks for women in your company and industry, or create your own.

There is a future with promises and opportunities waiting for you. All you need is concrete strategies for upward movement and options to move forward to experience clarity, synergy, community, connectedness, pride, and the power you desire.

Get the career and life that you want, without regrets.

A Life of Opportunity

I know it's possible to have the career you want because I did it. And over my career, I've seen other women do it too. I have mentored and coached hundreds of women as they've navigated their careers and entered positions of leadership. As a hiring manager, executive coach, and diversity and inclusion consultant, I've also assisted companies in creating equitable hiring practices, bringing hundreds of women into male-dominated companies, and equipping them with specific strategies to thrive.

By my twenty-seventh birthday, I was on the corporate-finance leadership team of a multi-million-dollar company with offices in over forty states and Canada. I've served in leadership roles on political campaigns, on the boards of directors for nonprofits, and on municipal government boards. My membership and leadership roles with organizations like the United Way of Greater Atlanta; with professional associations like the National Association of Black Accountants, Inc. (NABA), National Black MBA Association (NBMBAA), and Association of Certified Public Accountants (AICPA); and on the Alabama State University Foundation Board and the Percy J. Vaughn Jr. College of Business Advisory Council helped me develop valuable skills that I leverage in my career, as well as giving me the opportunity to give back to generations coming behind me.

I am dedicated to helping men and women succeed in their careers on their own terms and become better leaders. I work closely with global companies in financial services, healthcare, law, professional services, technology, emerging markets, federal and state government, and more, providing career strategy and leadership development training.

I've been coaching since long before I knew it was called coaching. It's humbling that people I've hired or worked with in the past call me when they need help with a salary negotiation or hire me to coach them through large projects, challenges, and transitions. I've provided career strategy coaching and designed career workshops for my corporate clients and the master's program at Robinson College, Georgia State University, and for NABA and NBMBAA. I've designed a six-week career accelerator for members of NABA. I also have a global career accelerator and career club for men and women who have decided they are no longer waiting on their managers to help advance their careers—they are taking matters into their own hands because they know what they want, and they are going after it.

When I think about the success of my clients, I'm proud to say of the hundreds of women I've coached since 2011, all either received a promotion or a new job with an average compensation increase between 25 percent and 40 percent as a result of applying the strategies I designed.

When I'm not working, you can find me serving as a volunteer in the community, co-hosting the *Before 30* podcast, sitting outdoors reading a book or magazine, listening to music and singing along, dancing, and laughing out loud with family and friends. I have realized the importance of seeking childlike wonder and embracing moments of joy in life, and I apply that philosophy to everything I do.

Now It's Your Turn

The five proven strategies that I share in this book work together to create a strategic guide for navigating the successful creation of your dream career—because it's not just about performing and doing the work. It's about having a plan and being strategic to get in the game that the men are already winning.

Learn how to design a career strategy that's tailored to you. Create a personal style so you can get noticed and maximize your earning potential. Increase your confidence and self-awareness so you can best perform at work and communicate your professional value.

I provide concrete strategies to help you take control and understand how the system works in your organization. When you understand what's valued in the organization, you know what your managers will reward you for.

A strategic vision provides you with a blueprint for your career, and that's what I'm sharing here with you: five proven strategies for success, fulfillment, and excitement.

It's a playbook of ideas, skills, and tools to help you accelerate your career (and your life) and to be unstoppable.

Chapter 1

OVERVIEW

"Never feel bad for being assertive, speaking your mind, and putting your foot down. What you think is anger, others see as a good solid display of self-esteem."

—*Alison James*

Business Is Moving—Can You Keep Up?

Women have made huge strides in today's workforce. There are more women in the workplace than at any time in human history. We are represented at every level of the business world, from administrators to accountants to managers and CEOs. Forty-four percent of companies have at least three women in their C-suites, companies are addressing pay equity, and flexible and remote working arrangements are helping to make raising a family while working a little easier than ever before.

Unfortunately, when it comes to succeeding in leadership roles, women still lag behind men. We make up roughly 7 percent of CEOs in Fortune 500 companies and only 10 percent of top managerial positions. The number of women in the workplace was impacted in 2020 when over two million women dropped out of the US labor force due to the global pandemic caused by the COVID-19 virus. Many of the women who left the workforce were working mothers who were furloughed, laid off or who opted out because it was easier to manage home and schooling without the stress of working too.

We know what we are facing and the toll it takes to decide to leave the workforce when we don't desire to. We have to respond to this crisis, reclaim those women, and establish supportive policies so women will not be forced out of the workplace again.

Women are a vital part of the profitability of companies; however, companies haven't yet established policies and cultures to support working women with children in the same way men with children are rewarded.

Men receive a fatherhood bonus from employers associated with stability, commitment, and deservingness, resulting in increased wages.

Women receive a motherhood penalty from employers associated with long-term instability, less committed, and unfocused, leading to lower wages and fewer opportunities.

And that's a problem, considering that 71 percent of women are in the workforce, many as the primary bread-winners for their households. Women have the solutions we are waiting on.

Communicate Your Value—No One Else Will Do It for You

When I was in the ninth grade, my mother was insistent that I learn how to type a minimum of sixty words per minute. She had big goals for me, but she, along with my typing teacher Mr. Wall, also believed that typing fast and accurately would be the differentiator in my career growth. It was for her, so I did it. I typed fast and accurately, and then came along spell-check—and it no longer mattered how fast or how accurately I typed.

This idea about typing was my first lesson in how to differentiate myself from my peers. Unfortunately, it was during my first college internship that I realized typing fast was obsolete, so I had to find and continue to find ways to set myself apart. What was the value I brought that was different from others, and how could I communicate it to my managers and clients, so they too saw value in it?

Break Free from the Norms

Too many women are bound by old societal and even cultural ideas about who women should be. Things are changing, and the roles that dictate what and who women can be are no longer limited in the ways they once were. But we still let those expectations limit what we can achieve.

As a hiring manager and executive career strategist, one of the things that I've encountered over and over is this misconception that women have about career advancement and the quality of their work. This idea that opportunities will come because we are technically competent and do good work is especially prevalent among women. Many believe good work is enough to speak for itself. We think that as long as we do our work and don't ruffle any feathers, someone out there will help us leverage and navigate our careers.

Well, I'm here to call false on that theory. The good work we do is the minimum, and it usually is only rewarded with more and more work.

Unfortunately, a lot of managers can't balance both managing and accelerating their careers as well as multiple other people's careers. Frankly, they shouldn't have to. It isn't the responsibility of your manager to solely promote the value that you create and to ensure that every opportunity or promotion that's available is brought to your attention.

It's up to us, as women, to take a more active role in navigating our careers. In order for us to see more women in senior and executive leadership roles, we have to take a more active role in communicating the value that we create in our organizations. We have to be constantly looking for new opportunities. We have to be in a relationship with more people at our companies and within our profession. We have to manifest the opportunities we want.

Embrace Your Ambitions

Women can take charge of their careers—so what's holding us back?

So many of us are held back by a fear of elimination. We work so well in a role (one that we've already outgrown!) that we're afraid to lose what we already have by striving for more. We don't want to disappoint our boss, team, or clients by leaving or moving up, and we don't want to let go of the feeling we get from obtaining mastery in one role to try something new that we may not be as good at.

The reality is that you need to identify the next role *before* you've mastered the current one, so you know what skills to foster to open the right doors for what you want next. You want deep mastery of your current role, but that gives you tunnel vision. You get stuck, and you don't plan the next stage of your career. You need to replace that tunnel vision with a career strategy. Know exactly where you're going and what you have to do to get there.

As girls, we are trained to play nice, be polite, follow the rules, do what we are told, wait our turn, and not skip ahead.

Assertiveness is seen as bossiness, and bossiness is seen as aggressiveness, and if we have aspirations, we're labeled as too ambitious. Men are rewarded for being ambitious and aggressively pursuing their career goals—it's reframed as focus and determination—while women are harshly judged and ostracized for the same traits and labeled hard to deal with.

After years of internalizing these stereotypes, we start to believe them, and we start to think that having a voice and speaking up is "unladylike." That is not how women should operate.

As women, we also sometimes use these stereotypes against other women. We are infected by these anti-feminist ideas that make us believe that if we take control and verbalize what we want, we will be perceived negatively. These beliefs run so deep that we don't just fail to fight them when men express them. We apply them to ourselves, and we use them against other women.

Those decisions about career and ambition are also complicated for women by the question of children. We often must make decisions about how far and how fast our careers can go based on the realities of raising children. We worry that the high-paying, high-visibility roles will be too demanding and a struggle to maintain if we decide to have children. We may even have to pause our careers because of family and parenting choices.

And if we make the decision not to have children, or if

we have children but pursue those high-pressure roles anyway, there's often a negative perception that we've put our careers above our families.

We need to allow ourselves the freedom to make the choices that are best for us without guilt. Guilt is a useless emotion that does not solve any of our problems. We can make the best choices for our careers without being held back by guilt and those deep, unconscious, sexist beliefs and social constructs. A woman's place in the world has evolved, and it's time for us to evolve with it.

In January 2021, the United States welcomed two incredibly powerful working women to the national stage. Our newest first lady, Jill Biden, is a mother who continued her career as an educator on top of her duties as a mother, wife, and then first lady. She sent a powerful statement to women across the country, and maybe even the world, that said, "I might not be able to have it all right now, but with the proper planning and the proper timing, I can eventually have everything that I desire."

Our first female vice president, Kamala Harris, has transitioned from the top attorney in the state of California to US senator and the first woman to serve as the vice president in US history. She is showing us that we can be a successful career woman, active family member, and a wife who's adored, respected, and cherished by a husband.

There are many examples out there to inspire us, and more will come. We will see more women moving into senior executive roles and still pursuing their other passions, whether that's motherhood, volunteering, business ownership, or supporting the career of a beloved partner and spouse.

It's the choice that matters—and the freedom to make it. It's up to us to decide what our paths will be and to communicate those choices proudly and without reservation.

I can relate to both Jill's and Kamala's stories. Like Kamala, I didn't have children of my own, but like her, I have an extended family I adore: my nieces and nephew are an active part of my life, and they look up to me and value my input and my place in our family. At the same time, they recognize the importance of a purposeful career and what service to others means to me. They have also witnessed the importance and the impact of caring for the elder members of our family. I have had to make choices on how to best manage my career and what I can have when, without regrets.

Getting Unstuck

I remember it like it was yesterday: every morning, my mother would put on a dark, sleek suit or a dress with a pop of color, delicate earrings, and red lipstick. She'd give me and my brothers instructions for the day and rush out the door for work, looking impeccable, her heels clicking down the stairs and to our long driveway. Her clothing was a trademark feminine stylish—it was her brand. I knew that was how I wanted to look when I went to work. I imagined myself as a business executive, wearing suits and high heels to work every day— and I did.

Early in my career, I had all the pretty suits needed to match my desire to look the part. The look went with my ambition to succeed, but I didn't have the know-how I needed. I completed all my tasks before the deadlines, without errors; I worked hard to be liked and attempted to build all the right relationships with my colleagues. But I kept running into the same stereotypical gender and race roadblocks about my ambitions and career goals.

So, I kept my head down. I did my work, collected my paycheck, and stayed clear of trouble. At first, I thought I could just stay in my lane, and I would be okay—but the truth was that I felt trapped. I knew I would be stuck if I fell victim to my current situation. The thing about ambition is it doesn't go away just because you push it down.

Playing small doesn't suit women who have big goals and who are destined for more.

Finally, a new opportunity made me realize that ambition was exactly what senior leaders looked for. I was offered a role that I wasn't looking for, I didn't know existed, and I didn't apply for it. If the role had been posted as an open application, I would never have let myself apply for it. I would have imagined the person who was best suited for the role, and I wouldn't have pictured myself. I would have disqualified myself by believing that I wasn't ready for a role so big—so visible. But out of nowhere, I was offered this new role, and I took it. And it turned out that I was more than ready for the role. I was perfect for it.

My boss was the second-highest-ranking employee in the agency, and he respected me for my ambition. He poured more ambition and drive into me. He challenged me with opportunities to make my career better. He mentored and sponsored me. He taught me how to make connections and build relationships upward, downward, laterally, and outside of the agency and my profession. He reminded me that I needed to always understand and be aware of the direction the business and industry were headed. He made me realize that I was the *only* person responsible for my success, and I had to take control of my career.

My confidence exploded. I was leveraging my skills to do new things, I increased my visibility, and I became unstoppable.

What Are Your Ambitions?

The skills taught in this book are a framework for your career, but the truth is that they're also life skills. I teach negotiation skills to many of my clients, but it's a skill I use in my daily life, even with a five-year-old! On a family trip to the Georgia aquarium, I was trying to get a picture of my nephew. Every time he saw the camera pointed in his direction, he said no and turned away like Idris Elba dodging the paparazzi. Finally, I knew I needed to try a different tactic. "Evan," I told him, "You've seen all of the pictures in my house, right? Well, if you let me take this picture, I'll put it up on the wall. Do you want a picture of you to stay on the wall?"

He thought about it and then grinned. "Okay!" he declared. As soon as he knew what was in it for him, he was on board. Just like a manager!

All jokes aside, I do mean it when I say that these are life skills. Yes, they'll help you become indispensable in the workplace. But they'll also help you transform your relationships and take charge of your daily life.

It starts with an outlook adjustment—stop asking for permission, and start going for what you want. Be strategic about the choices you make, ensuring that you're positioning yourself for the future. To further your career, communicate your value and make sure you're leveraging the impact you make.

Don't be afraid to take risks! That means taking on roles you're not ready for and learning through them. Master negotiations by leveraging your influence and speaking up loudly, and as you are moving to the top, help ensure the success of other women by forming your own girls' club.

As you get inspired and start your career journey, make sure to reflect on where you are now and where you want to end up. Then read this book and figure out exactly how to get there.

And remember to have fun while you do it!

Chapter 2

MAKE BOSS MOVES NOW

"There is no passion to be found in playing small—
in settling for a life that is less than you are capable
of living.

—*Nelson Mandela*

Boss Thinking

When you take part in important meetings, do you sit away
from the table—or at the table?

Mary, one of my friends, had a middle management
role in her organization. But when she was called to the
boardroom for meetings, she tended to sit in chairs *away
from* the table, not *at* the table. "In case I didn't stay for the
entire meeting," Mary apologetically explained to me, "I
didn't want to take up a seat for someone else."

She wasn't alone. In larger meetings, other women shied
away from the conference room table.

Her male colleagues, of course, would always go straight
for the table—sometimes taking away seats from more
senior leaders.

Mary was a leader, and people expected her to help drive the meeting. But she was literally removing herself from the conversation. This habit meant that Mary couldn't be properly seen, which hindered her ability to communicate. She often ended up sitting behind subordinates.

Finally, a trusted colleague pulled Mary aside and advised her to lean into her management role. She needed to stop sitting in the background and claim her space. Mary acted on the advice she got. She shed her soft-spoken, apologetic attitude and started thinking and acting more like a boss. She began sitting in a notable position at the table. She started speaking at each meeting, offering ideas and input. She confidently took her rightful place at the meeting table and immediately saw the results. People listened more to what she had to say, and subordinates treated her with more respect. This shift gave Mary the confidence to make other strategic moves and boost her stalled career.

Mary told me her story, and it immediately brought to mind all the women leaders I've worked with and coached who used to do the same thing: they would arrive early to a meeting, grab a seat in the back or farthest away from the most senior leaders, and take careful notes instead of participating. I helped those clients see that this passive, unassuming behavior disempowers them by making them invisible and puts a serious drag on their careers.

Many of my clients blame this passive behavior on being an introvert, soft-spoken, having an accent, or not knowing how to break into the conversation. Some don't want to say the wrong thing or ask a stupid question. So, they take notes and often end up doing more of the administrative tasks to support the "thinkers and delegators" on the team.

Regardless of the reasons, the results are the same. Their male managers give them performance feedback that they need to contribute more. During our coaching sessions, I learned they had a lot to contribute, and their questions were very smart, well-articulated, and innovative. They had the solutions but lacked the confidence to speak up.

Three prompts to break into a conversation:

1. Say their name: when you say the name of a person who's talking, they will stop speaking and look at you. Then you can begin to speak.

2. Make a big announcement: Say out loud, "I have an idea." It will get everyone's attention and allow you to speak.

3. Introduce your idea: Say, "Let's consider this"— and share your idea.

Boss Moves

When Mary put her foot down and started claiming her rightful space, she was making what I like to call a "Boss Move." This proven strategy involves putting yourself out there and getting noticed. Boss moves help promote your career goals and empower you to implement strategies to achieve those goals—and get noticed.

Boss moves draw attention to you and your greatness. They help you get unstuck and result in large career leaps instead of frustratingly small, incremental steps. When you make moves like this, you draw in others around you who are invested in your efforts and set yourself up for long-term career success. A lot of women are constantly looking for something else to fix instead of propelling themselves forward. If you don't step up and make boss moves, you risk getting stuck in an unsatisfactory or unchallenging role, missing out on opportunities for bigger roles, and of course, not getting paid what you're worth.

You can use specific techniques to make boss moves that will catapult you toward the career success you desire and deserve. Get noticed with the right kind of help, embrace your ambition, and be strategic. Ask the right questions, and build strong relationships with colleagues upward, downward, laterally, and outside your company.

Getting Noticed

My coaching client Kristine came to me because she was presented with the possibility of a promotion to partner. "It's finally my time," she declared. She wanted to show that she was ready for the gravity of the role, but after twelve years in her profession, she felt stuck in a worker role. She was constantly in the weeds, bombarded with *doing* detailed tactical tasks instead of developing and executing more productive operational and strategic tasks.

The barrage of tactical tasks Kristine handled each day included administrative projects like testing processes performed by staff, reviewing reports, scheduling, or pulling presentations together. These tasks stopped her from getting the same recognition as her male peers. When you are stuck working on a large number of administrative and tactical tasks, it overshadows your potential for the critical thinking, strategic planning, or leadership required for senior roles.

As her coach, I explained that while helping your staff is a good strategy for mentoring and moving projects along, it is not how senior leaders become executives. When too much time is spent on tactical tasks, it negatively impacts your ability to develop the skills needed to grow.

On the other hand, productive operational and strategic tasks allow you to demonstrate vision, build synergies across differences, generate more business, solve problems, and prove you're ready.

Kristine needed to focus more on operational and strategic tasks, such as planning and setting long-term goals, ensuring the team has resources, managing the big picture and ensuring the right teams are in place, and creating new products and services for clients. Her role needed to inform and determine the tactical task.

When you take on more operational leadership roles, you become a strategic member of a team that moves projects forward instead of just the person who puts the finishing touches on final reports. Strategic tasks give you an opportunity to articulate your knowledge of the organization's big-picture goals. With this heftier type of decision-making, you stand out as a key team member with great potential.

I helped Kristine see that she was bogged down in unproductive tasks. Although she had a leadership title, she kept doing work she should have been delegating to her direct reports. To get promoted, she needed to impress her bosses and show them that she was capable of bigger thinking. Together, we came up with a plan for her to create and identify a new stream of business revenue in a market her firm wasn't actively serving.

After twelve years of doing primarily the same task day in and day out, with small incremental changes, Kristine felt inadequate and unclear about her abilities. She was terrified at the prospect of analyzing her industry, identifying new business opportunities, and selling a vision for building her own practice to current partners. But she conquered that fear by embracing her boss energy. She knew that she could lead a team to take on new challenges and succeed. She just needed to make a boss move.

Kristine achieved partner in her firm and still manages the successful practice she had the courage to carve out. She developed a reputation for working hard—on the right kinds of projects.

When you spend too much of your career working on unproductive tasks, you lose. Even high-potential employees fall behind when their focus is on such tasks. They never develop the super skills that accelerate their thinking and propel their careers.

They get stuck and hit a plateau because they've been doing the same job, even with different titles, far too long. They don't interview well because they struggle to articulate their ability to take on a bigger role.

It's Okay to Be Ambitious

Certain words spark unfavorable associations in the minds of both men and women. For example, women who are openly ambitious are often labeled as difficult, aggressive, mean, and undesirable to work for.

Unfortunately, people view the terms "ambitious" and "aggressive" so negatively that they've become normalized as undesirable traits in women. But being ambitious doesn't mean you're a conniving double-crosser. It *does* mean you are clear and intentionally going after what you want. For career women, that means knowing where you plan to end up—and how you want to get there.

I strongly encourage my clients to embrace their aspirations. Women need to stop being ashamed about wanting success. Leverage your ambition! It's a positive force that drives accomplishments and keeps you focused on your goals.

Be authentically you: If you want to be the boss or make a high six-figure or even seven-figure salary, don't be ashamed. Go get it and be true to yourself in pursuit of it. Do it your way and be authentic to your identity. You don't have to be a man, and you don't have to act like a man, to be taken seriously. Remember, you can leverage your feminine energy to realize your ambitions.

Avoid false bravado or peacocking; it's a distraction and causes alienation. Make boss moves and achieve your goals while remaining your authentic self.

Own Your Ideas: One way to embrace ambition is to own your ideas. Too often, an idea that's casually mentioned during a meeting can be hijacked by someone else. Avoid this by speaking up and volunteering to own the development of the idea. If you are not comfortable with such a visible declaration, document your ideas. It doesn't have to be anything too formal—just organize your thoughts in writing, preferably in an easily sharable slide deck.

When the time is right, say to a colleague or your manager, "Hey, we were in a meeting talking about this, and I came up with an idea. Maybe you can help me talk it through." This establishes your ownership of the idea and allows you to informally recruit someone to openly support your work. It also gives you a chance to practice before pitching your idea to your leaders and the entire team. This approach shows management that you're interested in and committed to promoting the organization. It shows that you are a strategic thinker *and* have a vision.

Don't Wait for Permission: You are uniquely positioned as a woman to identify underserved or unserved markets—externally and internally. Who can you get your products and services to? How can you deliver them better, faster, differently than your competitors? I've seen women sit on great ideas because they're afraid they won't be taken seriously. Here's a key takeaway: *you don't have to ask for permission to present your ideas.*

Your ideas do not have to be perfect or complete, but they must be shared. Sharing your ideas is evidence of your critical and strategic thinking. You don't have to wait for someone to say "go" so that you can promote the future you want for your organization or yourself. Just go ahead and do it.

Avoid Perfectionism: Perfectionism is a hyper-focus on being flawless. It comes across as being overly picky and critical. Women far too often want everything to be perfect before they make a move. We want to make sure we have mastered *all* the skills on the job description list before we apply—leaving nothing to chance. We want to read and reread the draft of our pitch documents to ensure all the graphics, fonts, and colors are perfect. Perfectionism slows us down and paralyzes our ideas. That is one thing I admire about men. Since childhood, they have been proud and excited about all of their ideas, and they don't hesitate to tell everyone about them, even the unfinished or maybe foolish ones. If everyone within your company waited until an idea was perfect before sharing it, you might go out of business.

Men will apply for a job if they meet just 60 percent of the requirements; women wait until they meet closer to 90 percent.

We are literally screening ourselves out of the conversation.

Perfectionism is also the lens of our harsh judgment and criticism of others. We harshly label someone's unintentional one-time error as a reason to disqualify them for opportunities. We all want to do our best work, free from errors and with a level of excellence. But it's important to do a self-check to evaluate how your perfectionism impacts your ability to take action and how it impacts the people you lead.

Develop a Strategic Mindset

Executing boss moves requires a strategic mindset. You need to do these things:

1. Eliminate disempowering thoughts and behaviors.

2. Make your voice heard.

3. Remove the junk.

4. Challenge assumptions.

5. Be passionate about what you do.

Let's break these categories down in more detail.

1. **Eliminate disempowering thoughts and behaviors:** Stop apologizing! Stop saying, "I'm sorry," and stop asking for permission. Stop replaying mistakes and blaming yourself. Learn

from mistakes and setbacks, apply the learning, execute a new approach, and move on. Stop questioning whether you belong in the room. You do! Instead, embrace a big-boss attitude and confidently take your seat at the table. Bet on yourself and do what you know needs to be done.

Far too often, women are in awe of people we think are better than us. We start to tell ourselves, I don't speak as well as they do, everyone likes them more, and so on. We overwhelm ourselves with comparison and devalue our abilities (gifts and talents). We silence ourselves. Don't forget you were hired too. And no matter what people say, you were hired for what you can contribute to the team. Therefore, contribute.

2. **Make your voice heard:** Stop being sheepish: Before she was a chief executive for a global Fortune 100 company, Robin wasn't on the radar as someone who could run an entire organization. She was a reliable technical analyst, but she didn't demonstrate or vocalize an interest in a leadership role.

   One day, she was asked to bring reports into a meeting with senior leadership. Robin, a petite woman, tiptoed into the meeting with her head down—making herself small—and handed off the reports. Then without making eye contact, she quietly left the room. She thought she was doing the respectable thing and minimizing disruptions. She missed an opportunity to speak and be noticed. Instead, she thought her role was to be a courier. Her manager told her about leadership's concerns regarding her sheepish behavior. It was a turning point. Robin became more aware of her body language; she began sharing her thoughts without waiting to be asked and made her career ambitions clear. "I want to be CFO one day," Robin declared.

Stop waiting around for someone to announce that it's time for you to be promoted. Instead, make boss moves to advocate for yourself. Share your ideas, express your opinions, and make your aspirations clear.

At the beginning of a career strategy session, I ask all of my clients the same two questions:

- What role do you want to be in two years from now?

- Who knows you want that role?

If no one knows you want a particular role, how are they going to help you get it?

3. **Remove the junk**: Is your resume filled with lists of tasks you don't like doing? Far too often, we sell ourselves short by repeatedly highlighting tasks on our resumes that we've done but are not passionate about doing. And we are rewarded with more of those same tasks and similar jobs that don't allow growth. Just because you've mastered a task or skill doesn't mean you have to sell it. Remove those tasks from your resume and highlight the strategic tasks that will demonstrate your readiness for something more challenging.

4. **Challenge assumptions:** Women often stay in roles too long or allow themselves to transition to another role that's essentially the same thing because they don't challenge assumptions about their lack of career aspirations. This passive acceptance doesn't expose you to new experiences that drive professional growth. Instead, you need to speak up and ask for what you want. Challenge the assumptions others have made about your career goals and ask for more responsibility to do different things.

5. **Be passionate about what you do:** No one will know that you care if you don't say that you do. Make a plan to consistently communicate

your career goals to leadership. Failure to do this results in what I call "junior purgatory," where you get trapped in a junior staff role for years while you sit around waiting for someone to offer you a promotion or a pay raise. Thinking that your hard work will get you promoted is *not* how the game is played. Promoting yourself is how you get promoted. Show off your passion and make it clear that you're ready for the next step.

Ask for the Right Things

What organizational support do you need to strategically manage your career? Are you asking the right questions to get that support?

My client Malia is an engineer at a global tech company. Every week she asked her manager for feedback, and every week he told her how great she was. The more he said she was doing great, the more frustrated she was with him. Meanwhile, he wasn't talking to her about being promoted but was assigning her more work. Her career was stalled, and her frustration was increasing. During a coaching session, I helped Malia realize she was asking the wrong questions. "You're asking how you're doing at your current position, but what you really want to know is what's necessary for you to get to the next level. You're not asking him the important questions, the ones that allow him to give you concrete feedback and direction." Instead of repeatedly asking for performance feedback, she needed to frame the conversation around her career goals and ask for guidance on how to get promoted to manager. During a coaching session, Malia and I developed a promotion framework that would clue her manager in on her *true* career goals. She wanted authority to manage her own team and move from a tactical executer to an operational manager. The framework starts with gaining insight on the following:

1. What behaviors and skills are valued and rewarded—at your company, in your department, in the organization, and on your team(s)?

2. What is the career journey from your current level to where you want to be within two to three years?

3. Is additional training or more credentials required?

4. What is the average time it takes for high performers to get promoted?

5. How can the skills gap be closed in the shortest amount of time?

6. How can you take action, find opportunities to lead, or join a team on a visible high-stakes project that will demonstrate your readiness?

Malia worked with her manager on the five questions, and he identified a project he wasn't originally considering her for. He proudly recommended her for the role and pushed the team to select her. He moved from being her manager to being a sponsor. She is now off his team, making big boss moves, with increased salary, all within months of gaining a promotion into management.

Building Relationships

Boss moves involve building relationships with colleagues and leaders by understanding what's important to *them*— what do *they* value. The same psychological techniques you use to build trust and manage relationships outside of work can be successful in the work environment.

Once Malia knew what to ask for, her next struggle was creating the type of relationship she wanted with her male boss. She valued his feedback and wanted to develop more of a mentor/mentee relationship, but when she saw him interact with her colleagues, it was always as "one of the boys." She couldn't figure out how to engage with him in that way, so she shut down completely.

She gained a whole new perspective when I suggested

she ask herself, "If this was my husband, what would I do?" She'd never thought about it that way.

"I would ask him what he wanted. I would find out what was important to him," she said. It was a huge breakthrough.

"Now you've got it!" I encouraged her. "The psychology of working with men in the office is very similar to how we work with them at home—or in our friendships. You have to understand what's important to the person who's managing you and then create a relationship with them based on that."

The realization opened a whole new channel for her. She realized that feedback doesn't always have to be instructional and that she could approach her boss as a friend and equal instead of always seeking a relationship where he pushed her to grow and told her what to do. She gave herself room to have more fun, which in turn let her be herself. Their weekly check-ins became more conversational and less tense, allowing Malia to share her *real* career goals. This shift in communication, along with her exceptional work record, led to a greater personal understanding and a positive shift in their working relationship.

When you are clear about what is important to your leadership, and you refine your approach, you can make boss moves to accomplish your goals—and get what you want.

Mentorship and Sponsorship

Who's got your back at work? Who's speaking proudly and positively about you when you're not in the room? We all need someone to have our back and hold our trust in confidence. We also need someone with social capital who's highly regarded within our organization to speak up for us when we are not in the room.

I was very fortunate in my career to have a lot of men, mostly white men, stand up for me and have my back.

When I worked at Deloitte, there was one person in particular who I knew had my back. He was the only Black male partner in the Atlanta office. He was admired and respected in the firm. I didn't work for Avery, and at the time, I didn't think there was anything I could offer him in return, but I told him he was going to be my mentor . . . Yep, just like that.

Mentors are your safe place to land. They are the ear that knows the difference between when you are venting your frustrations and when you need advice. Avery was a good place for me to vent and get all the frustration, upset, and unknowing out. He would listen without judgment, and I knew he wouldn't repeat what I said. He would help me make sense of my concerns and laugh with me—and at me. I needed him in the workplace because he helped me think about the big picture, gave me the inside scoop on what it takes to be successful in the firm, and had nothing to lose by helping me.

Avery provided me with opportunities to demonstrate my leadership skills and expand my network to get noticed by firm leadership and within the Atlanta business community. He heightened my exposure by assigning me special projects like starting the Deloitte Black Employee Network (BEN), a business resource group for the region that included many offices.

Whenever I wanted to do more, get noticed, and leverage my skills, I had to tap into my sponsors. They were the ones in my performance meetings who stood up for me and did the blocking and tackling on my behalf. They, too, had my back, but there was something at stake for them. They were putting their names, reputation, and social and political capital on the line for me. My success was tied to their reputation—and their reputation was tied to my success. A sponsor is the person(s) who will vouch for your readiness. They are not necessarily involved in your skills development, but they will advance every opportunity that you want to get. My sponsors fought for midyear pay raises, larger bonuses, high-visibility projects, the best clients, and fast-track promotions on my behalf.

Once I learned how to leverage a sponsor, I never stopped tapping into them, even as a business owner.

In the next chapter, we'll explore strategizing for the future.

Chapter 3

BE STRATEGIC

"The most difficult thing is the decision to act, the rest is merely tenacity."

—*Amelia Earhart*

Aiming High

Having a strategy can make all the difference when something goes wrong in your job.

Tia was working in banking, and she wanted a change. She liked finance and wanted to help startups grow and scale. She is a natural networker, so she leveraged her ability to network and build relationships to get an interview at her dream company.

Unfortunately, because Tia was so new to the industry, she didn't understand the structure of the organization. She ended up taking a role whose listed job responsibility seemed perfect for her—only to learn that her new position was equivalent to a junior associate, two steps lower than where she had planned to be in the organization. And she was the only person in the global organization with this title.

Tia came to me because she was frustrated that her title didn't match her responsibilities.

A title may not seem important, but there's value in ensuring that your title demonstrates where you are in an organization. It might reflect on your compensation, and it will definitely reflect on what people assume your responsibilities are. You can argue that you're doing the work of a manager in a job interview, but you might not even get to that interview when your title says you're a junior associate.

Tia felt stuck. She thought it was going to be impossible to accelerate her career because she had mistakenly gone backward with her title. Would she have to leave her dream job for a new role with the right title at another company? No, but she would need a strategy.

I took Tia on as a client for six months. As part of our coaching engagement, I taught her how to demonstrate and communicate her value and readiness. We designed a communication plan to convince her leaders to retroactively change her title and simultaneously align her for a promotion in the same fiscal year. She was determined to reach the level of senior associate so that she would be eligible for an upcoming promotion to manager.

At first, the team showed resistance. "You're only a junior associate," they said. "We could maybe bump you

to associate, but you'd have to be a senior associate to be
eligible for the manager promotion."

Network like a boss

Would you like to crush it with networking?

Go to www.unstuckandunstoppablebook.com/action
sheets for a free download of "Learn How to Network
Like a Boss."

But Tia was armed with our plan and had concrete proof
of her accomplishments. When she met with management,
she stood confident in her request. "I've been functioning
as a senior associate for nine months," she said. "Here are
all the things that I've accomplished. My goal was to be at
a manager level within eighteen months of my hire date,
and I'm determined to apply for that promotion. I think
I've demonstrated that I deserve this title change so that the
managerial role will be open to me."

Tia's communication strategy included the following
items:

• Factual evidence of her accomplishments and
contributions to the business.

- Proof of her ability to master the business and create opportunities in record time.

- Narratives and feedback from clients about her outstanding work and value.

- A list of the quantitative and qualitative results from process improvements she devised that were adopted and deployed.

- Confirmation of the relationships and connections she brought to the company.

After reviewing the information Tia had compiled, management agreed. They retroactively changed her title to senior associate, making her eligible for the promotion to manager—which she then got.

For Tia, the key was to not just sit back and say, "Oh well, I messed up. I took the wrong job." She built a concrete strategy for fixing the problem, and armed with that strategy, she was able to prove her worth. She told her leadership, we all messed up. You guys brought me in at the wrong level knowing the skill and experience I had, and I accepted the offer at the wrong level."

When you're strategic, you position yourself for the future. You create a long-term goal and then break it down into the steps you need to take today to end up where you want to be. Instead of sitting around and waiting for life to happen, you make the first move. When you always know what's next on your career journey, you claim your power. You can be your best because you're going after that thing that fuels you. In this way, you ensure that your efforts aren't in vain, and you take advantage of the community that wants to see you rise.

Get Proactive with Your Career

You control your future. As long as you never let go of your plan, you have an unstoppable blueprint to get the career you deserve.

It doesn't matter who your manager is, what company you work for, or what industry you're in. The ultimate responsibility for navigating your career is *yours*. To do that, you must be solidly in the present with your eye on the future. That future should be realistic and balanced, based on the direction that your industry and your profession is going. Understand the impact business disruption, technology and innovation will have on your career. Finally, be mindful of the effect of your own life choices, like marriage and children or deciding to go back to school.

Too many women let life happen *to them* instead of taking charge. They wake up one morning and say, "How did I end up here? This isn't what I want to do!" I see this a lot with my clients. They start off their careers gung-ho in their twenties, but by the time they're thirty-five, they realize they've let the wind take them where it will, and they're lost. They come to me and say, "This isn't what my expectations were. This isn't what I want to do. I hate my job." They're disenchanted and searching for purpose.

Being strategic allows you to stay proactive, to never be in a position where other people are making decisions for you about your career, your direction, or what you should be doing. Being strategic also means having a vision for your life or for your career. A business doesn't run based on day-to-day operations; businesses run and grow and are sustainable because they're constantly looking at the future. They have a vision and a mission statement, and they adjust their goals based on market and customer demands.

As individuals, we need to have that same strategy in managing our careers. We should always have our eyes on what the future may hold for us, even if there are some unknowns.

The Key Elements of Strategic Planning

The first step in planning your career strategy is understanding where you are in your career and your specific role. Are you functioning more tactically, operationally, or strategically? Whether you're managing people or you're an individual contributor, knowing the difference in these three mindsets will help you understand where you are on your career journey, what is most important in your role right now, and how you can move toward your goal.

Keep in mind that for some people, these divisions can be fluid. You may be simultaneously acting both tactically and organizationally, for instance. Determining your role is meant to give you a guidepost for where you are, but don't see this as a box you're trapped in.

Tactical

Tactical roles are typically entry-level or occur within the first two to five years of your career. When you're in a tactical role, you're focused primarily on becoming an expert and having a deep understanding of what your key job responsibilities are.

These roles are very performance and action-oriented. You want to become an expert in your job responsibilities, so you do whatever it takes to achieve that. For example, if you're an accounting professional or an auditor, it's important for you to understand the foundational fundamentals of accounting and auditing. On a tactical level, you need to know what your company's methodology is, what your clients do, how they make money, how your company makes money, and how your role specifically fits into that.

From there, you start asking what your responsibilities are as a staff auditor and how you can excel in that role. You determine the day-to-day functions and responsibilities of the role, and then you break those down to understand how your role supports the overall company vision. If you're client-facing, you also have to understand how the products and services that your company offers support your client's business.

Operational

If you're a business or industry expert, your role is operational. You've probably been in this industry or with this company for five to nine years. You're starting to move into greater leadership responsibilities, both with people and the business itself. You could be a project leader or a department head, but you're definitely focused on how the business functions and how all the pieces fit together. You're probably more involved in the long-term planning of how to grow the business.

Strategic

How long it takes to move from organizational to strategic roles depends a lot on the structure of the organization. By the seven to twelve-year mark, you should be expecting to move to the next stage of your career. When I look back over my own career, I was probably becoming more strategic after six years.

By the time you hit a strategic role, you're an industry

expert. You might not be a CEO or CFO, but you're definitely in a middle or senior management role. To deliver and manage your role responsibilities, you're probably sitting at the table for all the conversations and deciding how every function of the organization works together. You're setting the vision, you're communicating that vision to others in the organization, and you're totally responsible for both crafting goals and ensuring that they're achieved.

The strategic piece is where you start to go deeper in your profession and really understand how you can leverage the knowledge you've accumulated to navigate your career. You understand where you fit within your current organization on a deep level. At this point, you should be having more conversations about your contributions within the organization or be looking at other companies that might need your skills and expertise.

How do these elements apply to you?

As you move throughout your career, you need to be very clear about what percentage of your role is tactical, operational, or strategic because it defines the expectations others will have for your output. What are you being evaluated on, and what does the organization value?

You have to understand the culture of the organization that you're working in. To me, there are two levels to what's valued: what the organization values overall, coming down from the C-suite, and also what's important to your manager, the person that you report to. You need to align your game plan with both of those things because we're rewarded and evaluated based on what's important to others in the organization, not what's solely important to ourselves.

I've had a lot of clients who thought they should be rewarded for certain things they did, but no matter how great those things were, they didn't align with what was valuable or important in the organization. For instance, I have clients who mentor others in their organizations or teams. That's a really valuable and selfless task, but is it important to your manager? Does it help you get promoted? Or is it a nice-to-have that you do just because it's important to you?

Knowing the difference is critical as you begin building your five-step strategic plan.

Get Where You Want To Be

One client I helped with a five-step strategic plan was Diana. She worked in global consulting, and she had left an employer for a better opportunity. Now she was interested in returning to that first company, but there was a catch. She was determined that she would return not as an employee but as a senior executive. But when she expressed that desire to her old colleagues, she was told that she simply didn't have the experience. She would need to start as a director and work her way up. She was told that no one comes back at that level without working their way back up.

Diana had a huge goal, but her experience didn't yet match that outcome. She wasn't ready to take that plunge. She knew there were some things she would need to do in order to get to her goal, but she didn't know exactly what they were. That's why she came to me.

Together, Diana and I wrote out her end goal and then created a five-step plan to get there. This was helped by the fact that she knew exactly where she wanted to end up— not just the role, but the company. Her goal was simple. "To return to the company as a senior executive, without starting at the director level and working my way up."

I showed Diana a five-step process to chart her goals: self-discovery, career exploration, professional development, leveraging skills, and pursuing goals. I'll go into each of those steps later in the chapter, but here's how Diana employed each one.

First, I asked her some honest questions about who she was right now and where she was currently in her career. This self-discovery phase focused on what was missing right now and what she needed to accomplish. During her career exploration, we talked about the promotions that were available in her current organization. What would she need to do to make a boss move? What types of clients would she have to work with for her old company to value those connections? We charted out the next three years of her career at her current company.

Next up was professional development. This stage was all about visibility: Was she quoted in anything? On what industry conference panels had she been a subject-matter expert? Was she taking on leadership roles that were considered prestigious—president of a professional association, for instance, or board seats? She saw how those things would be valuable to put in her portfolio for the interview process and created a two-year plan to increase her visibility. She also decided to get an executive MBA. While she could have received the senior executive role without it, it certainly raised her value.

Diana did a lot of work in financial services, working with large financial institutions and investment brokerage firms. She leveraged her skills to bring in huge clients, which created a big win on her resume. The work she was doing was spotlighted at her company and within the financial services regulatory industry, which earned her two promotions within two years. She demonstrated her leadership abilities both in her job and in a volunteer board-leadership role, both concrete things that she could show to her potential next employer.

By the end of those four steps, we had mapped out a four-year journey to take Diana from where she was to where she wanted to be. The final step was both the simplest and most difficult—sticking to the plan. She pursued her goals with single-minded determination, and when she eventually decided to start conversations about a role at her old company, she was welcomed back in the exact role and level she desired.

She succeeded in the pursuit of her goal because she had a clear and concrete strategy for the future, and she wasn't afraid to do what it took to follow it. You can build your own plan using the same five steps I used with Diana.

The Five-Step Strategic Plan

Here are the five steps for building your strategic plan:

Self-discovery

Know thyself. I always tell the women (and men) I'm working with that they should have their hand on the pulse of what's important to them and who they are throughout the different phases of their careers. Who you are and what is important in your twenties is very different than in your thirties, and again in your forties. We are impacted by our life events, work experiences, and the choices we make.

That's why the self-discovery phase is something you should redo on a regular basis. Take the pulse of what's important to you, and allow that to shift and change over time.

The key to self-discovery is identifying your core values. It's vitally important to check in with your core values, understand how they align with the work you're currently doing, and take stock of how you demonstrate and experience them within your organization. A lot of times, people get burned out or frustrated with their companies because their core values are misaligned with what they're doing.

Your Core Values List

You can go to www.unstuckandunstoppablebook. com/actionsheets to see a full list of core values that might apply to you:

Core Values Exercise

Identify your top five core values, and then check to make sure that your integrity aligns with those things. Are you living those out? Are you experiencing them both in work and life? We can't compartmentalize life and work, so it's important that they're present in every part of your life.

Once you've established your core values, you need to understand how they apply to your goals. Ask yourself, "What's important to me right now?" Let's say your answer is a promotion. How does that align with your core values? If one of your core values is achievement, then promotion is probably important to you. What does that look like? How often do you need to be promoted to be happy? Are you being identified for promotions? Are you seeking them out? Are you demonstrating that this is important to you? If you're in the same role for five years and achievement is important to you, you'll end up feeling undervalued, discontent, and frustrated without knowing why.

The thing I always emphasize to clients as we do this exercise is "know thyself." Don't shy away from who you are! Be honest, and make sure you're taking the time to really look within yourself.

Career exploration

If self-discovery is all about you, career exploration is all about where you can go in your career. What are you interested in? What companies or industries interest you? Where do you want to go? Take a really big step back and ask yourself how the skills and training you have might relate to completely new opportunities. There will be jobs in the future that do not exist today—and jobs today that will not exist in the future.

A lot of people don't take a broad enough look at the different industries and professions that they could access by leveraging their education or skills. Because you've been in the quick-serve restaurant industry for ten years, it doesn't mean you can't leverage what you know in a different industry.

There is no limitation on where you can take your career.

There was a time when people would spend their entire careers at one company in one profession, but that's no longer the case. You may not be an expert by industry standards, but you can be an expert at leveraging your specialized knowledge and expertise, and you can do that in a new industry as long as you're prepared to put in the time to learn. I've had clients move from healthcare into technology, from professional services into motion picture entertainment, and from banking into consumer goods. The sky's the limit.

This is also the right time to examine the various structures of the companies you're interested in working for. Like Tia, who didn't fully understand what position she accepted, it's easy to get stuck when you don't have a firm grasp on your prospective company's corporate structure. When you do decide to move, make sure you're going in at the right level.

Professional development

This is an area that a lot of people overlook as a very valuable way to position yourself for the future. Being involved in a professional association or pursuing professional education, either internally at your organization or externally, is essential to accelerate your career. It's great when companies recognize the importance of growth opportunities and provide training, but sometimes we have to make that investment ourselves. That might mean paying for membership dues, training fees, or conference attendance.

We're in a culture right now where there's a plethora of both free and fee-based training. Take advantage of those opportunities at every turn! Joining an industry association and attending monthly meetings, conferences, and conventions is a great way to hear about what's happening in your industry. What are the big disruptors? How is technology changing the game? Where is the industry growing or shrinking in unexpected ways? This is also a great way to network. Having relationships outside your company allows you to start dropping seeds—"This is what I'm interested in; this is where I want to go"—because the next great opportunity might not be with your current employer.

Leveraging skills

As women in leadership, we have to speak up. We cannot be afraid to use words like "I" and to say, "Yes, I did it." I know . . . I hear you . . . you don't feel comfortable talking about yourself, so you say "we"? If you don't feel comfortable saying what you did or where you were instrumental in leading the team, can you guarantee that someone else will? We can't be afraid to tell our stories and acknowledge the value and successes that we've helped our teams, employers, and clients achieve.

Your Super Skills List

Do you know your super skills?

You can download a free list of super skills at <u>www.unstuckandunstoppablebook.com/actionsheets</u>

Saying "we" all the time will overshadow your individual contributions and abilities. It makes it vague and unclear what you did and can do. Leadership needs to be able to quickly identify key employees based on successful performance—what they can do. You want everyone to specifically know what you can do. Communicating what you have done is also the best way to overcome objections during your performance review and when asking for a raise and promotion.

Leveraging your skills is about being a one-woman public relations team and marketing strategist for yourself. You have to share, in a way that you're comfortable with, the value that you bring. Share your ability to be strategic, to be a visionary, and to solve problems with those super skills you have.

When it's time to list your accomplishment, do you have to think long and hard about what you've done over the past twelve months? You may be like me, doing so much that you can barely remember what you accomplished in the last six months—let alone the last twelve to twenty-four months. I'd like to encourage you to create a brag book. That way, you won't have to be awkwardly trying to look back, saying, "Oh, two years ago I did something like this . . . ," but not being able to really remember. You need to document everything. Keep a spreadsheet or notebook where you list the successes you've had on specific projects, your contributions, and the specific skills you leveraged and developed during those projects.

When you look at job descriptions, you can then say, "Oh, I've mastered this already. I have stories that I can share both verbally in meetings and on my resume."

Your Success List

Start tracking your success!

You can download a free template to do this at <u>www.unstuckandunstoppablebook.com/actionsheets</u>

Pursuing goals

The previous four steps should increase your confidence, expand your network, and demonstrate that you can increase your value and leverage your skills and do so both faster and more strategically. By the time you get to step five, you have a clear understanding of the things you need to be successful and get where you want to go. You should feel assured that even with marketplace competition, you're the best candidate for the role you want.

You can pursue your goals because you know what you've done and you feel comfortable about what you want to do next. Pursuing your goals comes naturally once you have a clear vision of what you need to do.

One important key to pursuing your goal is to verbalize it. Make sure you're totally clear about where you want to go, and what you want to do, and tell others.

Then go and be unstoppable!

Planning for the Unexpected

Part of positioning yourself for the future is acknowledging that some things are unforeseeable. Some of these are positive, some are negative, but in all of them, there's an opportunity. You have to make sure that your plan is flexible enough that you can change your priorities and decisions when circumstances change. Staying on top of changes means constantly working on your plan and updating and refreshing it.

These are some scenarios that have impacted my clients during their career planning:

1. You accept a position with a different company.

2. You are unexpectedly assigned a new manager with your current employer.

3. You accept a promotion or lateral transfer with your current employer.

4. You are laid off, downsized, or otherwise terminated from your employer.

5. You choose to leave the workforce for personal reasons, with plans to return.

6. Technology changes your role, and you have to upskill.

7. You decide to change your profession (e.g., leaving teaching for engineering).

8. Circumstances force you to make a career move before you plan to do so.

When one of the above happens, the general rule is to go back to step one. Figure out which of your five steps are being impacted by this change. Are your core values still aligned? Do you need to pursue different professional development opportunities? What has changed on the ground?

If you were unexpectedly assigned a new manager in your current workplace, for instance, the first thing you might want to do is go back and look at leveraging your skills. Your first meeting with him or her should be about your contributions to the department and the value you bring. When you can do that, you can continue to strategically pursue your career path and ensure that all your decisions are deliberate and calculated for the best possible outcome.

In the next chapter, we'll go over how to leverage your impact and communicate your value to set yourself up for career success.

Chapter 4

LEVERAGE YOUR IMPACT, COMMUNICATE YOUR VALUE

"A lot of people are afraid to say what they want. That's why they don't get what they want."

—*Madonna*

If a Tree Falls in a Forest and No One Sees It, Will You Get a Raise?

You may fear that growing into leadership threatens your boss. But the right leadership personalities welcome your growth and abilities. In fact, they will demand it.

I had a client, Jazmyne, who was referred to me by her employer. Her boss saw a lot of potential in her but felt that he couldn't get her out of the worker-bee mentality. During our first meeting, she told me how unfair it was that she wasn't being identified for growth opportunities.

"Do you ever communicate the value and impact that you bring to the team?" I asked her.

She sunk back into her chair, shutting down. "Oh, I couldn't do that," she said. "My parents taught me not to be a braggadocio." That was the word she used. "People who brag about themselves are arrogant and a turnoff. No one wants to be around someone like that."

"Can you share with me one example where you missed out on something because you were silent?" I asked her.

Jazmyne didn't even have to think about her answer. "There was a project that I really wanted to work on that would have given me a lot of visibility with leadership. But I didn't tell anyone how much I wanted to do it— I thought if it was for me, I would get it. And someone else was selected."

Sidenote: This isn't magic. If it's for you, you must GO GET IT!

"Had you been speaking up for yourself and not wishing for destiny, what would you have gotten?" I asked.

She shrugged. "I think I probably would have been selected for it. I have the right experience, and I have been working on similar things."

"So would it have been bragging to tell someone you were the right fit?" I asked.

"No," Jazmyne admitted. "I guess it would just have been . . . advocating for myself."

Once she had reframed bragging as self-advocating,

Jazmyne got more comfortable with the idea of doing it. We came up with a value proposition for her to engage in relevant and clear communication in a way that didn't make her feel she was being disingenuous or talking herself up too much. For instance, one phrase we practiced was, "We were able to accomplish XYZ, and my contribution to this accomplishment was ABC."

Armed with a new strategy, Jazmyne started regularly raising her hand and communicating what she wanted. She put together a strategic career plan for herself and stopped relying on others to be her sole career advocate. By communicating her value and leveraging her impact, she got the recognition and promotions she so badly wanted. During the eighteen months that I coached her, she was promoted twice. Today, she's a vice president, with more responsibility, more compensation, a lot more visibility, and she's much happier.

Being able to leverage your impact and communicate your value is your currency to success. It's how you create social capital, how you move up, and how you define your worth both to yourself and to others. It's about being your best and showing people the value of having you as the leader on their team. When you learn how to let yourself shine, there is no obstacle, no barrier, and no situation you cannot overcome.

Behind Door No. 1 is Exposure

According to many leadership professionals and hiring managers I consult with, how well you do your job has very little to do with how successful you are in your career. A key element to success is exposure.

The book *Empowering Yourself: The Organizational Game Revealed* by Harvey Coleman says that exposure is the most important component of success. According to Coleman, 10 percent of your success is determined by how well you do your prescribed work, 30 percent comes from your brand or image, and an astounding 60 percent results from the exposure you receive at work.

Wow! This may be a mind-blowing revelation for you if you believe that error-free, perfect hard work will speak for you. As your coach, I'm here to sound the alarm and call false on the idea that all you need to do is perform your job well.

As a former hiring manager, I recall that management discussions regarding promotions and succession planning typically start with someone in the room putting forth a candidate's name for consideration.

My first thoughts weren't usually about whether the candidate was any good at performing their job (I assumed they were; otherwise, why would anyone put forth the name?). Instead, I and others immediately jumped to wondering what we knew about them (i.e., their exposure).

Below are a few questions that come to mind when considering candidates for promotion:

1. Do I know what they've done or accomplished?
2. How often have I interacted with them directly?
3. Have I observed them in a high-stakes negotiation or presentation?
4. Have I heard others talk about them before today?
5. How visible (vocal) are they in the office and in meetings?

Although you can receive incremental pay raises and promotions without significant exposure, it will not be sustainable, and you are guaranteed to fall below the market value of your peers if you opt out of this very important element of success. The more people who know you in the performance consensus meetings, the easier it is for them to agree to your promotion.

Let's talk about what exposure looks like in the remainder of this chapter.

Your Impact Must Be Visible

Companies are looking for people who can make a difference. They want changemakers—or maybe even rainmakers. They're looking for people who can make the business as a whole better and more successful. You need to communicate not just how great you are but how you can make their revenues higher and their clients happier.

One way to do that is to have a brand that expands beyond the internal walls of your organization. You want to be *known*. You can, and should, leverage your impact to create social capital not only within your organization but also within your profession and industry. This is something that a lot of people don't do well—especially women.

Most of us are known only within our own department or group, or at best, throughout the company. We may have a few relationships and synergies across departments, but it stops there.

When you expand that influence further, you create a competitive advantage. People who are "known" are seen as valuable influencers in their profession, and that value sets them apart. It's important to provide added value, especially now when the market is so competitive. As I often say, "there are a ton of people out there doing what you do. They have the same credentials, the same education, and similar on-the-job experiences. So what sets you apart?"

Once you determine your competitive advantage, you

have to be able to communicate that advantage continuously and regularly (but not obnoxiously!).

The Power of Language

When I coached Jazmyne, one of the things we worked on was the distinction between bragging and self-advocating. One of the areas we focused on is the difference between "I" and "we," and using "I" when it counts.

Great leaders brag about their teams, but at the same time, they have the ability to identify and stress their personal contributions. Women have been traditionally wired to think in terms of "we." You need to know how to effectively go between being collaborative but also identifying how you helped make the whole process work.

Another way language can be used against women leaders is the negative association behind terms like "ambitious," "passionate," and "strong." We have to take back our power by reclaiming those words. If they call us ambitious, we embrace that. If they make our passion about emotions, we confirm how much we care. If they say we're strong, we ask how that could possibly be a bad thing.

At a recent conference, I spoke about how women have to be comfortable in the spotlight, even while having the choir behind us. It's important for us to be comfortable speaking about our value and contributions without the shame of being too ambitious or driven—or braggadocious.

Remember, there's an appropriate amount of tooting your own horn that's not just encouraged but *necessary* for you to be visible within a large group of very successful people and high performers.

So why do we have so much shame around being self-aggrandizing? Where does that come from? Think about moments where you felt uncomfortable talking about yourself. Was it because you were told that it wasn't an appropriate behavior for women? Did you see it in men and find it uncomfortable or even off-putting?

We need to fight those unconscious responses. Men win because they tell you how freaking great they are even when they're not. It's time women had the same unshakeable confidence.

What I find in a lot of people I coach is that they already know they should be talking themselves up, but they're not doing it. They see it as a success tactic for someone else, but they can't quite motivate themselves to take the plunge. I help my clients become more comfortable as their confidence grows using a few exercises discussed in this chapter.

Not everyone is super ambitious or concerned about looking smart and great. However, as a coach, I can help them formulate words that align with how they ideally want to be seen. In that way, they talk themselves up authentically but still powerfully.

So what are the key components of an assertive,

positive-impact campaign? You need to understand your skills and center of influence, and then create a unique brand.

Make A High-Value Introduction

Your introduction is more than your name and title. In less than sixty seconds, convey your value and expertise.

Low value: My name is Kimberly, and I'm a software engineer at AWS.

High Value: My name is Kimberly, and I'm a Principal Software Engineer at AWS with five years in emerging markets and three years on our global team serving clients in a variety of industries, including healthcare technologies, automotive, and professional services. I have extensive knowledge about AWS solutions, and I am looking forward to working with you and using my expertise to provide you with superior services and solutions.

Understand Your Unique Skills and Traits

My client Nikki had to get a clear grasp of her skills when she decided to change careers. She was an auditor at a multinational professional services network, and she was incredibly good at what she did. But she was starting to hate her job—she wanted to do something more purpose-driven.

Nikki volunteered at work to assist with the company's diversity and inclusion (D&I) initiative, and she decided that she wanted to move into D&I full-time. But she had no idea how. Together, we strategized how she would communicate her value during the hiring process. We focused on aligning her skills and experiences to the value that she could create for a prospective company.

She was incredibly good with people, and she loved developing processes and procedures. We knew these would both be huge parts of any position in D&I. She was able to find specific examples of times where she had used those skills and figure out how to align them to what would be needed from her at her prospect list of companies. We packaged her lived experiences with her learned experiences, along with her self-starter attitude and ability to manage across differences.

Soon she was ready to apply for jobs. She found a perfect match, a brand-new role as vice president of diversity and inclusion in the motion-picture industry. With the confidence born of the prep work we had done, she went into that interview and laid it all on the table. She matched her skills to the qualifications they were looking for and showed how she fit the position through her skills, if not her experience.

They loved her, made her a contingent offer on the spot, telling her she was the strongest candidate over some with more day-to-day experience.

To leverage your impact, figure out what you're really good at and what unique and intrinsic value you bring to that thing. For me, my unique skill was that people had fun working with me, and I could see what others were *really* good at before they did. As a result, my teams did great work, we met our deadlines, and we were profitable, but we never lost sight of making it a joyful experience and allowing people to work in their zones of genius. It was hard work to keep it so positive, but it was worth it.

Often the things that are extremely valuable to our managers are the skills that keep the business going, but we overlook how we do those things. They become so much a part of our day-to-day routine that we don't see them as being unique. It's important to take a step back and ask, "What do I do well, and that I do differently or better than anyone else?" Then find ways to make sure people know you're good at those things and you do them regularly.

Understand Your Center of Influence

One thing that sets you apart from your peers is your circle of influence. Who supports you – maybe even inspires you? Who can validate the value that you bring? Who is on your side? Your circle of influence is the people around you who are telling your story. They are respected, trusted, and well-known. That could be your manager, influential mentors within your organization, and direct sponsors. It also includes peers who speak highly of your work. You need to cultivate a strong circle of influence.

Cultivating a strong circle of influence starts with finding a good mentor, someone who can step up and help lead and develop you. I didn't seek out most of my mentors in a formal way—they found me when I did good work. But if those relationships aren't developing on their own, you need to take charge and seek them out. Remember how I told Avery he was going to be my mentor. Pick them. Good candidates are your managers or those in leadership, but make sure you're targeting the right people with solid reputations with a few "boss moves" you can model. It can't just be a job for them—they need to take pleasure in helping you develop.

Your Personal Board of Directors

Mentors are sometimes called a personal board of directors. The individuals on your board of directors should be like a stock portfolio—diverse. Consider the following to make up your board:

- Men and women
- Different races and ethnicities
- Mix of ages and generations
- Different experience levels
- Different industries and professions
- Different relationship statuses
- Different employment types—employees and entrepreneurs

and other aspects important to you.

Keep it diverse so you can hear different perspectives. You may find that you'll discuss certain topics with one mentor that you do not discuss with others.

Not all managers have the level of emotional intelligence to direct and guide people. Some simply aren't interested, and others have too many direct reports to single you out for special treatment. But if you have a relationship where

they're identifying opportunities for you, keep them as part
of being in your center of influence. Let them know that
you consider them a mentor and work to strengthen that
relationship.

Another important part of your circle of influence is
your peers. The peers in your circle of influence are either
modeling themselves after you or telling other people
about your value. If you're lucky, they are doing both.
When your peers are part of your circle of influence,
they don't feel threatened or have a sense of direct competition with your work. There's a false perception that
there's not enough room for everybody. This false perception creates a practice of self-preservation, an unfriendly
competition that creates a toxic work environment. The
circle of influence is a demonstration that there is enough
room, and opportunity, for everybody to be successful.
Creating this support system around your success is really
important.

Your center of influence is the community that supports
you and validates the value that you bring. They've seen
it, they've witnessed it, and they've benefited in some way
from it.

I call them the band, but I also think there's a component of ambassadorship to it. They have a vested interest in
your success that is equivalent to their own. They're willing
to speak up and speak out on your behalf, and even talk
about you when you're not in the room.

They're a trusted group, but they don't appear out of nowhere. It's up to you to grow your circle of influence— and to reciprocate for others.

Create a Relevant and Clear Brand

I have an exercise I do with my clients: they have to describe what they are known for in only three words. In one minute, they have to describe the value they bring to their organization. For a lot of people, creating this brand story can be a huge challenge.

That was true for my client Jessica. She wanted to make some big changes in her department, but she was finding it challenging to get space at "the table." She worked in a male-dominated IT department, and she was spending a lot of energy trying to blend in, to be "one of the boys." I told her, "Beige is boring! You need to stand out."

Jessica was preoccupied with being likable and afraid of being labeled as overly ambitious, but I knew she couldn't keep ducking the spotlight if she wanted to effect real change. In order to succeed and move up, you have to get the attention of the people above you. That means embracing your ambitions. I asked her what her three words were.

"Fixer," she said immediately. "Innovator. Planner."

"Do you think, right now, you're showing that in your work?" I asked.

She realized she wasn't and that she couldn't be afraid to

be seen for who she was. She wanted to effect change, and that meant letting people see her passion. Jessica started to communicate her accomplishments, to speak up in meetings and advocate for herself, and socialize her future goals. For her, part of being daring was doing both what she was hired to do and tackling new problems she identified.

With her new brand firmly in place, she became known as the office fixer. Soon her opinion was being sought out before she even had to speak up. She was the one that leadership sought out when a difficult client conflict or matter needed softening.

What are your three words? What do you think people would say your words are? Is there a disconnect between how you see yourself and how others perceive you? If they use a different word, is it a synonym to what you said, or is it wildly different? In this exercise, your goal should be for others' perceptions to align with your own—and for multiple people to be using the same or similar words to describe you. That shows that you have an authentic brand and consistent performance and that you're not acting in a disingenuous way just because you think you should.

This is not about being likable, and I want to stress that, especially for women. Likeability is an important component in leadership because people tend to follow people that they like and trust. But being liked isn't the only factor that's important. Identifying your three words is more about being consistent in the areas where you do your job better and differently than others in the organization. It's your brand proposition.

This ties back to the self-reflection component of the five-step strategic plan. You should know who you are, but other people should also be able to communicate that same image back to you. If they can't, then you're not demonstrating the values that you claim are so fundamental to your personality. You do not need to promote your brand. It should make itself clear through your actions.

If you don't know your three words or are unclear about your brand, go to www.unstuckandunstoppablebook.com/actionsheets and download the worksheet.

It's Your Story—Tell It

Earlier in this book, I encouraged you to tell your story and reminded you that you cannot rely solely on your manager to brag about how fabulous you are. We all must do it ourselves. And not just verbally but also in writing.

Why does this matter? Because women are losing at sharing their stories.

Women list fewer skills on their resumes and LinkedIn profiles than men. According to a 2021 study by Talenya (https://www.talenya.com/exploring-the-recruitment-pipline),

white men list an average of seventy-five skills on their public profiles, compared to sixty-eight for Asians, sixty-three
for women, forty-seven for Black/African Americans, and
thirty-seven for Hispanics. Women are simply writing less
text describing their careers and achievements on their
resumes and profiles.

This directly impacts your job prospects. The Talenya
study also shows that women's profiles list on average 34
percent fewer skills than those of men. It's no wonder
that men are receiving a higher number of invitations to
interview and are getting more job offers—which results
in more men in management even though women have the
same skills and experience.

Ladies, let's start the Power of Seventy-Five movement
and start saying and writing seventy-five adjectives in
descriptive sentences about our experience and skills. If your
resumes and experience profiles on platforms like LinkedIn
are sparse, recruiters will overlook you as a viable candidate
– or they will contact you about roles beneath your abilities.
You have to ensure your online profile and resume are rich
with content in order to catch the attention of the recruiter
who's looking for a reason to contact you. Don't be afraid
to talk yourself up.

Promoting your skills can be scary. That's why in the
next chapter, I'm looking at the importance of master
negotiations.

Chapter 5

MASTER NEGOTIATIONS

"Let us never negotiate out of fear. But let us never fear to negotiate."

—*John F. Kennedy*

Get in the Driver's Seat

Did you negotiate the salary you're earning today—or accept the offer at face value?

When I left a government job to join a corporation, I didn't negotiate the initial offer. It was so much more than my old salary; it felt like a windfall. I thought, *Whoa, look at all this money I'm going to be making.* Plus, I didn't have a whole lot of knowledge about negotiating compensation. I trusted that my compensation was in line with the role and my experience level.

It didn't take me long to realize that simply wasn't true.

I started asking questions and learned that some colleagues on the finance team who had the same level of experience as I did or even less were making $20,000 more per year than I was. That's when I went in and boldly asked for a raise. My communication strategy was to ask, "Why do I only make $70,000 per year?"

"That was the salary you accepted," the CFO answered me.

"With my experience and responsibility, I think I should be making at least $92,500," I said. To my surprise, he agreed and gave me a pay increase. Immediately. No questions asked. In fact, he agreed so quickly, I realized I might not have asked for enough. He also apologized that his predecessor underpaid me.

At the time, asking for more felt unreasonable. But negotiations involve give-and-take. You shouldn't walk in and lay your final offer on the table immediately. What appears unreasonable is where negotiations should start.

Women typically fail to negotiate compensation. In fact, 76 percent of women regret not negotiating an initial offer of employment. Many avoid negotiation out of fear, lack of knowledge, or a view that negotiation is unpleasant and uncomfortable. But negotiation is part of life! Even outside the workplace, we negotiate—when we shop, when we make plans with partners, and even when we want our nephew to let us take his photo at the aquarium.

I help clients recognize negotiation as an everyday occurrence—something to get comfortable with. I like to think of negotiation as a muscle you need to build and exercise. Mastering negotiation puts you in the driver's seat—of your career and your life. It gives you the ability to have whatever you desire for yourself. You can go after it because you're able to influence people and situations to support the career that you want.

What is Negotiation?

Negotiation is, simply put, a mechanism for getting what you want. Negotiations are high-stakes conversations that drive positive results during a career discussion. A successful negotiation results in a win-win for all involved parties.

If you don't negotiate, someone else is making decisions for you. They will make assumptions about what's important to you that may not accurately reflect your concerns or be in your best interests. You risk being overlooked or getting stuck with an outcome that falls significantly short of your career goals. You don't win.

When you master the art of negotiation, you feel empowered, your voice is heard, and your positions are clear to others in the room. You're far more likely to benefit when you drive the conversation. As you know, because negotiation is a give-and-take, you may not get everything you want. But the only way to ensure your voice is heard is to take a seat at the table, buckle up, and speak up.

You can become a master negotiator. This is my master course.

Be Prepared

Any good negotiation needs preparation. This applies to discussing compensation, hammering out contract details with a client, or determining team assignments with colleagues. You'll need to prepare in several areas:

Have a Communication Strategy

First, outline your key communication strategy. I typically walk clients through a series of questions to help them prepare for any important business conversation. Your answers become your communication plan.

- **What outcome will make this conversation or meeting a success?** I always suggest beginning with the end in mind. When the conversation ends, what's the ideal outcome? Do you want an agreement? Increased compensation? Approval to proceed? Write down what will constitute a successful negotiation in your eyes.

- **What are the best alternative outcomes if my primary outcome isn't achieved?** Chances are, you won't get everything you ask for. This is *not* failure. Be prepared for that and know what compromises you're prepared to make. Master negotiators envision worst-case scenarios and prepare acceptable backup outcomes.

- **What do I want to convey upfront?** High-stakes conversations can generate nervous tension, so your communication strategy should involve identifying a few key points to convey early on. For example, you may want to express why something is important to you or establish how all sides can benefit from adopting your point of view. A key to mastering negotiations is understanding "What's in it for me?" from all angles.

- **What is my point of view?** When you outline the rationale behind your desired outcome, you create a position statement. For example, if you're heading into a salary negotiation, you need a target salary goal and a clear argument about why you are worth that amount.

- **What documentation and examples can support my position?** If you're trying to convince, influence, or persuade the other party, arm yourself with good supporting documentation. If the conversation is about compensation, demonstrate the value your work has brought to the organization. You might gather performance metrics, emails from satisfied clients, or recommendations from colleagues.

- **What questions can I ask to drive the conversation?** Prepare some thoughtful, open-ended questions to learn what other people are thinking. Find out what they want. Understanding another's perspective is key to helping them understand yours. What can you ask to induce the other party to state their position and perspective?

- **Who can help me prepare and practice?** Identify a colleague or confidant who can help you practice in real-time and provide constructive feedback to fine-tune your delivery.

Maintain Composure

What if the conversation doesn't go your way? Can you react to disappointment professionally? I advise clients to express, not suppress, their emotions. If you're passionate about something, it's okay to explain what you feel and why.

The trick is in *how* you express that passion. You never want to lose your composure during a negotiation—the workplace still has a double standard about emotional and hysterical women. A man can demonstrate strong emotion, even use profanity, and people will brush it off. Professional women are not generally granted the same leniency for emotional outbursts. It's not fair—it just is.

Maintain your composure and be careful that your explanation doesn't come across as personal. I like to remind clients about one of Don Miguel Ruiz's four agreements: Don't take it personally. Not getting what you want isn't a personal attack. Expressing your viewpoint while maintaining your composure displays calm in the face of adversity. Keeping your cool will *always* enhance your professional standing.

Be Aware of Body Language

As you practice with a friend or colleague, pay attention to your body language and posture. Are you making eye contact? Are you sitting or standing squarely (not leaning or slumped)? Are you speaking firmly?

Voice is really important too. It's okay to be polite, but mastering negotiations requires a firm tone. I've helped many women who were naturally soft-spoken find their "negotiation voice." It takes courage and practice to get the right balance of assertiveness, volume, and pacing. I encourage my clients to practice out loud, sometimes in front of a mirror.

Get Your Timing Right

Timing is key in every negotiation. Be aware of outside factors before you go into negotiations. Is the organization positioned properly for what you want? Is now the right time? You want to identify what timing and circumstances are required to get a yes. During the negotiation, you can also note what timing might move a no to a yes and position you for a win down the road. You can respond to a no with, "Okay, if this doesn't happen now, can we circle back and revisit this?" Then it's up to you to ensure that the timing is right and all required pieces are in place when you revisit the point.

Take the Wheel

Master negotiators naturally take the driver's seat. Listening is important, but you want to keep driving the conversation. One good strategy is to let the other party know certain items are non-negotiable. You can do this by communicating the things you want to see happen that are most important to you—your desired outcome. This is when you use your negotiation voice.

I am in constant negations with clients and vendors. It's so regular that I don't really think of it as negotiation until I begin to state my non-negotiables. During this part of the negotiation conversation, I tend to slow down my pace. I start to use a tone that is clearer and more concise. I like to use what I call "the list." When I want to ensure things happen, I list them using numbering. For example, I might say, "These are the four items that

I want to make sure I get." And in order of importance, I list them.

What should you do if you reach gridlock on a particular item? If you realize a certain point is not likely to get to yes, don't cave in and automatically accept no. Keep your hands on the wheel and see if you can steer the conversation to a maybe. A key negotiation mantra is "No doesn't mean never."

Salary Negotiations

This is one of the most common workplace negotiations and one of the hardest for women. Compensation negotiation is critical because the pay gap only gets worse over time. Being underpaid early in your career can compound quickly, making it harder to catch up. For women who are the primary caregivers to their children or who have parental caregiving responsibilities, the numbers get worse due to the "motherhood penalty." This penalty plays out in the form of benevolence when others show consideration for your "situation" bypassing you over for opportunities because of the perceived burden it would have on you because you're a mom. You can end up in a situation where you are hundreds of thousands of dollars behind your male counterparts because of missed or never-presented opportunities.

Women tend to sabotage themselves when it comes

to salary. I know this is true because even when I've told clients, friends, and mentees exactly where to start their negotiation, they reduce it and lowball themselves. I received a call from a friend who was looking for someone to join his organization. He trusted me to send a strong candidate, and he'd hire them. I had one in mind and called her up. She was excited about the opportunity and wondered what she should ask for in terms of compensation.

I told her she should not go under $70,000 plus a performance bonus starting at 15 to 20 percent. She initially said okay, but after our conversation, she started to think about what a huge pay jump that was going to be for her after coming from a not-for-profit. She didn't want to seem greedy, and she got cold feet. When she received the offer, it was lower than what I had told her to take. She called me, and I pushed her to make a counter offer. She did, but not as high as I had told her to. Of course, they accepted immediately. Weeks and months later, she called me and admitted her regret, saying, "Women really need to learn how to negotiate compensation confidently."

Nearly all men negotiate their compensation, regardless of race and ethnicity—which contributes to the gender pay gap. Remember what I said a few chapters earlier? Men always think their value is great.

The US Census Bureau confirms there has been no significant progress in closing the gender pay gap along racial and ethnic lines between 2018 and 2019. The pay gap for white women remains at 79 cents for every dollar white men earn. The chart below shows the breakdown by race and ethnicity:

The Wage Gap	
All women vs. all men	82 Cents
Asian women vs. white men	87 Cents
Black women vs. white men	63 Cents
Latina and Hispanic women vs. white men	55 Cents
Native American women vs. white men	60 cents
Native Hawaiian & other Pacific Islander women vs. white men	63 Cents
White women vs. white men	79 Cents

*Note: White refers to white, non-Hispanic women and men.

I advise clients to reflect on why they shy away from negotiating compensation. Ask yourself these questions:

- How do you think the impact of not negotiating your salary could affect the pay gap over the life of your career?

- Why have you avoided these conversations? Is it because they make you uncomfortable? Or because you truly believe all offers are fair and equitable?

- Do you trust that everyone with the same experience and credentials is offered the same pay for the same role?

Overall, most people don't believe they're fairly compensated. According to the 2020 Compensation Best Practices Report by PayScale, 76 percent of employees believe their organization doesn't pay them fairly. When asked if they feel fairly paid by their employer, "yes" answers break down like this:

White men:	24 percent
White women:	19 percent
Black/African American women:	18 percent
Hispanic women:	19 percent

People, especially women, don't know how to bridge the gap between what they currently earn and what they believe they should be paid. On the employer side, there's not enough transparency to allow people to know what's fair. Most companies have significant flexibility about the pay range for a particular job. This means that there is usually room for negotiation. It's important for job seekers to understand who's making the offer—the hiring manager or a third party, such as a recruiter? If possible, you want to negotiate with the hiring manager who knows the allowable pay range and is authorized to make decisions.

One Key Question

I give my clients *one key question* to ask when negotiating compensation. Posing this question will ensure you get the best offer based on your value, skills, and expertise. You'll see how powerful it is in Jessica's story.

Jessica was an HR professional who took time off to care for a child with a serious illness. I helped her prepare to return to the workforce. She was up for a senior role and was concerned about being out of the game for a year.

In her field, staying up on current trends in the marketplace is vitally important. When she went for her interview, she addressed the gap by highlighting her past accomplishments, expertise, and her ability to learn quickly. She framed taking time off in a positive light; she was coming back to the marketplace refreshed and ready to roll. She also communicated that she had kept in touch with her profession by doing some advisory work during her leave.

Further, she openly shared the reason for the gap—to care for a sick child. Fully recovered, the child was back to school, and Jessica could refocus on her career. She sacrificed a year of work to be a good parent. Who wouldn't relate to and applaud that? She turned what she originally thought was a liability into an asset. Jessica was offered the job, but not at the salary she wanted.

To negotiate more, she popped the big question: "What do you need me to demonstrate to ensure that I'm at the top of my pay range?" This is my "game-changer" question that many people do not know to ask.

She realized there was something they hadn't heard yet or some perceived gap she needed to address to get a better offer. She leveraged her past experience, providing relevant examples to address their concerns, and then she impressed them with a detailed action plan to hit the ground running. Jessica wanted to up the offer by $20,000, and she got an agreement for $15,000.

But she wasn't finished. Jessica really wanted to get that last $5,000. In one of our coaching sessions, I asked if they offered a signing bonus. She hadn't thought of that. She went back in and asked if they could meet her $20,000 target with a $5,000 signing bonus. Presto! She got it—every penny she carefully and persistently negotiated for.

When you're asked what your salary requirement is— say it. Don't be coy and beat around the bush by being vague. The salary negation is part of the interview. You will be informed if your asking amount is outside of their budget for the position. How you manage this conversation informs the hiring manager of your ability to handle a high-stakes negotiation on their behalf within the company and with vendors and clients. The salary negation is part of the determination process.

Negotiation techniques are so important that you might want to learn more about them. Podcasts, books, and courses can help you learn and adapt strategies to fit your style and personality. The more you master negotiation, the more in control you are of your career, your finances, and your destiny.

Keep An Eye on the Future

When negotiating your salary, keep in mind that you're not negotiating based on your current role. You've already earned that salary! Negotiate based on the requirements and responsibilities of the new role.

Just imagine, if I had never renegotiated my salary, it could have led to me being underpaid throughout my entire career and never catching up. The long-term consequence of that for many women is over $1,000,000 loss during their careers. Renegotiating my salary was the beginning of my developing the skills to negotiate, and I'm glad it happened in my twenties.

When Exposure Meets a Negotiation

What would you ask for if you had an audience with someone who could give you anything you desired? Would you make a boss move? One of my clients had such an opportunity, and she spoke up.

Roz is what I call a "badass." She's valued for her leadership—she's daring, she's savvy, she's building a network, and she's all about making boss moves.

She, along with many other professionals where she works, was asked to share her insights and experiences about cultural issues related to being Black in America—specifically, racism and race relations at work and in the larger community they lived in. Many of her colleagues declined for personal reasons, but she thought to herself, "If I want to impact change, then I must be a part of the conversation, no matter how uncomfortable." It was a personal choice that evolved into a boss move.

Roz participated in a forum in front of the company's chiefs, the executive leadership team, and other senior leaders across the global organization. She caught the attention of many of the leaders for her candor, actionable ideas, and solution-oriented responses. A female executive in the company reached out to Roz for a one-on-one conversation. During their talk, the leader asked Roz what she wanted to do next. This opened the door for her to negotiate her next move.

Roz was prepared because during our coaching sessions a year prior, we outlined options for her next boss move. Roz knew to always be ready for this conversation, and the exposure had opened the door for her to go after what she wanted. Twelve months after a previous promotion, Roz moved from managing a team of sales engineers to being the global director with oversight of a multi-continent team.

She was in the right place—received exposure and spoke up at the right time—for successful negotiations. Roz leveraged her relationship with senior leadership, expressed what she wanted, and realized you couldn't get what you want on your own.

In the next chapter, we look at how women can better support one another in the workplace.

Chapter 6

GIRL POWER

"When women support women, amazing things can happen."

—*Viola Davis*

I Got Mine!

Have you ever admired a leader in your company and were then shut out or shut down by them—and it was a woman?

Sometimes the ones we admire most hurt us the most. When it comes to managers, women can be more competitive and territorial than men. My client Sophia lamented, "I try to support my manager, but I feel like she always shuts me out. I think she's intimidated by my knowledge."

Sophia had been struggling to connect with her manager, and the trouble was growing. "I get the impression she thinks she has to outperform every other woman in the firm or she'll lose her status. She appears threatened by other women, especially anyone who might be smarter, younger, or more efficient."

Over and over, I've heard stories similar to this. Many

successful women refuse to open doors for female colleagues out of a perverted sense of self-preservation. They adopt an attitude of "Hey, I made it on my own—other women can too." Maybe they've forgotten how hard they fought to get where they are, how lonely and demoralizing fighting alone can be, and that no one makes it on their own.

Organizations have plenty of room at the top for women leaders. If you want to work together and help each other, you need to invoke girl power.

"Girl power" is banding together to help women achieve executive roles, expand leadership opportunities, and create a pipeline of women ready to fill those roles. Many women who make it to top leadership positions mistakenly believe there's only enough room for one or two women in high-ranking roles. Their sense of self-preservation kicks in, and they refuse to help other women follow in their footsteps.

This creates a toxic environment of women not wanting to work with other women. It limits leadership opportunities, keeps women leaders isolated, deprives organizations of the contributions talented women can make, and slows down the promotion and advancement pipeline.

As women, we need to help each other open doors and succeed. We need to become active champions and allies for each other. When we do that, we create our own community and surround ourselves with others who want to see us rise. Even if we fail, we can fail in a supported way and demonstrate that women can work for one another and with one another. We can all get what we want, and organizations and companies will be better for it. Our efforts aren't in vain, and together we become both unstuck and unstoppable.

In this chapter, I share a vision for harnessing girl power to break the glass ceiling. Instead of fighting alone or amongst one another, we can rise and thrive together.

Creating a Girls'/Women's Club

Statistically, very few women make it past the middle-manager role. Organizations don't identify women early for senior leadership and executive roles, and many women don't speak up to pursue greater challenges. That's because there's no one out there advocating on our behalf. Men have an unspoken boys' club. Women need to design their own club, both formally and informally.

Within an organization, creating a girls' club can start with mentoring. Be the first one to take a stand, and more women will follow your example and participate as mentors and sponsors in the workplace. Even if you're not an executive, you can step up and select people to help develop.

I will say that many women are under-sponsored and under-celebrated. We need women to speak up! We need advocates for this movement.

Another way is to start building relationships. It can be as simple as reaching out to the most senior woman in your company. Build a relationship with her and see whether she's open to participating in bringing women together. Your company may have women's leadership initiatives as part of a diversity and inclusion program that you could help promote. You might find the beginnings of a girl-power group there.

I've seen women come together to create a strong voice within an organization. As they gather momentum, they attract more senior female leaders and, eventually, supportive men. People start to talk about their goals and experiences in taking on more challenging leadership roles. These stories help other women find the courage to follow suit.

One of the most powerful experiences of my career occurred because of the women I worked with at Deloitte. We had a high number of women managers and senior managers. Within the groups of women, we had a supportive network of Black women across service lines. It was an informal group, but we became friends, confidants, cheerleaders, vacation buddies, and "hype" women for one another. We helped each other prepare for high-stakes conversations, worked on clients together, bragged openly about each other's skills, and so much more. It was the first time I knew that working with and for women was possible and positive. As managers, we actively mentored and prepared the women who were coming up behind us.

If you can't build a girls' club within your company, turn to industry peers. The best place to look is professional industry associations. Connecting with other women in your discipline is an amazing way to build camaraderie. You can develop a safe network, build skills, and forge meaningful ties with successful leaders.

And while sharing stories is a good start, going further is critical. We need to provide each other with strategic, constructive feedback. Pointing out mistakes has little value unless it's accompanied by clear, proven steps to success. Women need to exchange concrete best practices and advice: this is what you should do, and this is how you can lead, communicate, or negotiate.

I also see value in creating a group of women across a variety of industries. Ultimately, you want your girl-power group to expand beyond your organization to encompass women across industries. Start by finding people you went to college with. This might lead to creating a more formal women's group that meets regularly to share progress, support, and knowledge.

Women are fighting for leadership opportunities in nearly every profession. Uniting and helping each other is the way for more of us to win big.

Changing Perceptions

In addition to opening doors and helping other women develop professionally, we need to fight the misconceptions that hold women back. These include the perceptions that women can't handle stressful roles and that we're constantly distracted by the demands of motherhood and family. These false ideas make us hesitate to go after promotions. They adversely affect how we interact with one another in the workplace.

Women's initiatives and formal diversity and inclusion (D&I) programs can fight these perceptions head-on. They can even set goals for promoting women into leadership roles or high-performing individual contributor roles. Informally, women within an organization can develop a consciousness that recognizes the need to see more women leaders and a commitment to support them. We have to "lift as we climb." Let go of thinking there's not enough opportunity for other women to participate in leadership, and instead actively find ways to make sure everyone has a seat at the table.

Research proves that women managers and leaders improve and enhance nearly all organizations. Companies are more profitable when women are in roles from director to executive leadership. Women leaders bring innovation, collaboration, and inclusion. They display natural managerial and conflict-resolution skills. They leverage emotional intelligence as a powerful tool in the workplace. What is there not to support?

Some women face additional challenges, and we should keep our eyes out for opportunities to address those imbalances.

Women and Race

All women face gender barriers, but I believe race and ethnicity create even bigger challenges. I've found that Asian American and South Asian American women are rarely offered mentoring and are left out of the professional female community. Even now, in the twenty-first century, some women face stigma when they break with cultural traditions.

Hispanic and Latina women are marginalized and fetishized as being bubbly and fun, but they are often not taken seriously or considered highly intelligent, which leads to being overlooked for leadership roles. The stereotype that future motherhood will take them out of the workplace is also a factor.

All too often, we hear Black women being labeled as angry and combative. Negative, theatrical stereotypes make their way into the workplace, including conversations about affirmative action that imply that Black women were promoted to fill quotas rather than based on their capabilities and contribution. Such stereotypes are particularly detrimental when it's time for promotion and managers overlook the woman's high levels of education, credentials, and experience.

Who made up these false stereotypes? And why do they persist?

These stereotypes persist because not enough women are vocal in debunking them.

A huge number of non-white women didn't get the right education to navigate their careers or haven't found a way to gracefully disengage from the cultural fabric of older generations. Career success is hugely important to these talented young women. Sadly, most of them have no idea how to attain their professional goals. That's why the fight against social and cultural norms shouldn't be waged only by women of color. It's up to every woman to be aware of this extra layer of complication and reach out when they see their peers struggling or being isolated.

When Your Industry Is Male-Dominated

Women are the majority in most offices and workplaces and the minority in leadership roles.

Every leadership position is male-dominated, but there's an extra level of complication when your entire industry is a boys' club. I've conducted numerous workshops for women in technology and seen firsthand how challenging it can be. Many of the women I worked with had questions about development, how to design a mentoring program, and how to create a safe group of supportive women. They faced serious barriers to advancing in their organizations.

I helped a lot of those women design their professional career plans. They identified specific skills to acquire and studied ways to expand their spheres of influence. I showed them how to build and practice leadership skills in a safe place within professional associations. We put together coaching plans that identified areas of professional development to get them on the right path. Above all, I taught them to stop seeing bosses as a primary career-management resource. Instead, they built girl-power alliances.

They leveraged those alliances to research fair compensation, identify promotion strategies, and learn other career-navigation tools. Eventually, they saw that working in silos was hurting them. Relying primarily on men for insights didn't align with the career path of their dreams. Post-workshop, it was wonderful for me to see these women pursue professional development strategies and start or join women's groups. As their networks expanded, they acquired leadership skills and confidence. They adopted the attitude, "It's my responsibility to navigate my career."

Most importantly, they realized they could champion

other women to build stronger leadership pipelines in their profession.

Disqualifying Her

During a meeting with a global financial services firm in Delaware, we were discussing inclusive leadership. Specifically centered on increasing the number of women in senior management roles, it was the second small focus group in a round of four with employees who were middle managers. During this particular focus group, the majority of the participants were women. The focus group shared statistics, barriers to entry, blind spots in the interview process, and talent identification and hiring. During the talent identification and hiring discussion, the word "qualified" was used multiple times to describe requirements for women who could potentially fill the openings. "She must be qualified. . . . We need 'a qualified candidate' . . . We must make sure she's qualified," everyone agreed.

I love being a consultant because I was able to wait until they all came to a consensus, and then I asked, "Do you have a practice of hiring unqualified candidates?" The room was quiet. After a few seconds, a woman spoke up in embarrassment because they had fallen into the gender-bias trap.

Ladies, we, too, must be aware of the language we

use when discussing one another. We perpetuate the negative-qualification stereotyping of women. We must see women as competent, viable candidates for leadership—and stop disqualifying them by using words we do not use for male candidates.

This is why I've been so excited by the increasing number of women CEOs of Fortune 500 companies. While the number is less than 9 percent, this year, we've added two Black women to the ranks: Rosalind "Roz" Brewer is the CEO of Walgreens, and Thasunda Brown Duckett became the CEO of TIAA. My desire is, when more women rise to the ranks of CEO in companies, we will discuss them differently—more powerfully. And I wish the same for women CEOs and Founders who create and grow their own businesses.

Overcoming Girl-Power Resistance

Not all women champion leadership pipelines or believe in girl power. I was consulting in an organization that had the goal of getting more women into executive leadership. We started designing programs and looked for female leaders to get involved. But when we reached out to a woman executive, she responded, "I don't understand why we need this. I got through all the BS around here. I made it. Other women can do it too."

This is *not* what we had in mind!

Did this woman forget about the toll taken by fighting battles alone? The devastating effect on physical and mental well-being? Had she felt the loneliness and isolation of being the only woman in the room, struggling to have her voice heard? The attitude of "I did it, so can others" is a disservice to other women.

We have to adopt the boys' club mentality. We need a spirit of active support—of teamwork—and we create a stronger team by supporting individual members. We need to create work environments that foster women leaders and that include women openly supporting the career advancement of other women. This means we eliminate microaggressions, microassaults, and negative judgments about fellow women. And we replace it with actively making recommendations for upcoming roles, defending one another during performance-consensuses meetings, making introductions, and passing along one another's names. We join each other's "one-woman" PR teams so we are not marketing ourselves alone.

We didn't convince the reluctant executive to join us. But we didn't allow her attitude to discourage us. Other young leaders in that organization signed up to be the voice of change. They put themselves out there. It wasn't easy. We heard leaders ask, "Are you going to serve your clients, or are you going to be the leader of women and Black people?"

To create sustainable systemic change, you must to

do both—serve your clients and champion others. That is the only way more women are promoted and stay with the organization. Women's retention improves, specific goals are achieved for how many women receive annual promotions, and organizations see an amazing, steady increase of women leaders.

Together, women can experience the transformative effects of girl power.

Becoming a woman leader and empowering the next generation of women leaders brings a new level of growth and challenge. But it's worth it.

Chapter 7

BE DARING

"Make your breaking point your turning point."

—*Dennis Kimbro*

Don't Wait for Mastery

Don't let career fear stop you from going after what you really want. Often when people aren't as daring as they could be, it's because they're dealing with imposter syndrome—that voice in their head that tells them, "You're not ready. You don't know enough. You haven't worked on these sorts of projects or done this kind of work."

You need to feed the opposite voice inside you—the cheerleader, the daring boss chick within. Let it speak! "You've got this! You can't move unless you take a step. At least try!"

When women look at a job description or hear about an opportunity, the first thing they tend to do is check the list of requirements: "I've done this; I've done that; I haven't done that." If they haven't done even 10 percent of the things on the list, they'll disqualify themselves from pursuing those roles. Sound familiar?

One of the things I want to impress on you is that a job description is a wish. It's a best-case scenario, and employers are often going into interviews prepared to get less. The whole point of the interview is to communicate about potential gaps in your experience and then explain how your existing skills will fill those gaps. If you wait until you have 100 percent of every list of nice-to-haves, you *will* slow down your career trajectory. You'll end up trapped in junior-leadership purgatory with ten years of experience, watching people who've been with the company for less time pass you by.

If you look at a job description and it says you need experience in fifteen areas, and you only have experience in nine of those, you only qualify for 60 percent of what the employer wants. So how can you make up for that huge 40 percent? First, look at the things you've done, not just what your core responsibilities are. Include skills gained through volunteerism and special projects within and outside of your organization. How have those experiences built the skills that they're looking for? How many of your skills can be translated? You may be surprised how qualified you really are.

In terms of how many of the requirements you need to go for a job, it comes down to a personal decision. But I tell my clients, "If you've got what it takes to do the tactical part of this work, to understand all the day-to-day responsibilities, then you can learn the operational aspect as you go. The strategic aspect is the one least likely for many candidates to have, so that's where you want to leverage your other experiences."

What if you *are* missing some of what you need? Don't let that be a closed door. Examine what pieces are still missing, and see what you can shore up. Can you take a course to fill the gap? Take on a new volunteer position? Even if you're a year out from moving into that job, you can use that job description as a roadmap for what you need to do to narrow the gap. Remember, you don't need to hit 100 percent. You just need to make yours a competitive application.

That isn't to say that mastery is not important or valid. Knowing the core competencies of your profession is incredibly important. You don't want to embarrass yourself by jumping in totally unprepared. But too often, we let that fear that we're unprepared—or someone else is more qualified—hold us back when really we're more than qualified to move into a role that requires more responsibility and more oversight. You don't want to constantly make small, safe, lateral moves. It's those big leaps that help us grow.

Be daring! Find opportunities, work on a project that pushes you to grow, and you'll also find yourself having more visibility inside your company. Opportunities will start to open for you externally in your profession, not necessarily to take a new job, but to be a thought expert. Your social network—and your sphere of influence—will expand.

All kinds of things hold us back from being daring. It's up to us to confront those fears with an open mind.

Keep in mind, it's not a growth opportunity if you already know how to do it.

Five Strategies for Your Future

I want you to stop asking for permission.

That's the heart of each of the five strategies we've learned together. The earlier you learn this in your career, the easier it is to incorporate it into your strategy. I attribute these five strategies to my success today, but a huge part of that success was not waiting for someone else to give me the okay. When there's an opportunity that's right for me, and it's aligned with where I want to take my career and the experiences I want to have, I don't wait for other people to tell me to go.

You shouldn't either.

I use these concepts when coaching women in business across all industries. My success in the corporate world certainly came because of these particular skills: always looking ahead, understanding where my profession was going, continuously finding opportunities to leverage my skills and take on bigger roles, and not getting complacent about where I was or even complacent about the positive feedback I was receiving. I made these strategies part of every day, and that's what you need to do. Continuously demonstrate your value to your clients and stakeholders, constantly communicate it, and remind them what you bring to the table.

I would have never moved out into entrepreneurship had I not developed confidence, a network, been a self-starter, and had the ability to perform. Had it not been for mastering these five skills and having a network of other successful women to support me, cheer me on, and even correct me when I was wrong, I don't think I would be where I am today.

Making Boss Moves

I had the guts to follow the path to my true calling.

When I first jumped out into entrepreneurship, I used these five strategies to gain the confidence and the network to pursue this new career successfully. I wasn't completely prepared for business ownership, but I had enough confidence in my abilities and my knowledge to get started at 80 percent and learn the missing 20 percent as I went.

I realized I had mastered my role when I closed my first half-million-dollar-a-year deal with a large manufacturer. This client didn't know me; I wasn't leveraging an existing relationship. They took a chance on me. I was able to demonstrate, just from the services I provided to large Fortune 500 companies, that I had what they call "the receipts."

First, I met with two members of the executive leadership for drinks and did my pitch. I met them on their ground—they were drinking martinis, and I drank one right along with them, showing my capable, smart, and fun sides. We ended up coming to verbal terms that night.

They ended up staying on as my client for four years.

How I Help Women

I work with professionals in a variety of ways, including both high-performance one-on-one executive coaching and larger women's coaching groups that focus on skills development and acceleration. In each case, we look at both career planning and career navigation. I help organizations and corporations design leadership development programs for their high performers, as well as for potential leaders who may need their performance to be enhanced so they can continue to be valuable in the organization.

If you're interested in participating in a women's group, visit my website and sign up. You can join the club, hire my firm for one-on-one executive coaching, or even schedule a time to talk about how we can help your company design programs for its employees.

What's Next?

You read the book. You did the work by downloading the supplemental worksheets, and you're armed with the five strategies you need to apply and incorporate into your career planning. So, what's next?

I want you to sit down and start putting a plan together to begin actively and proactively build your career around these concepts. As you transition into being a person who's confident and able to communicate the value that you create, you'll find the ways in which that value takes people by surprise. It's not the status quo.

Never work with your head down, expecting to be rewarded. Look up and identify how to leverage your skills. Identify the positions and roles that you're not ready for, and then boldly take the steps you need to take so you will be ready when it's time to move.

If trying to apply these ideas in your current organization seems daunting or maybe even impossible, I want you to remember that *you are not alone*. Success happens in community. It isn't all on your shoulders, and there's enough room for all of us to be successful. We must work toward the success of other women. We have to hold one another by the hand. Sometimes we may have to push, pull, and carry one another—but it's up to women to ensure the success of other women.

This is one of my core beliefs: success isn't about how

fast I get to the top—it's about how many people I bring along with me. I wouldn't have been successful or able to learn these five skills without the community of men and women who supported my career, who were my cheerleaders, my mentors, my sponsors, my advocates, and most importantly, who paved the way.

They opened the door, but I had to walk through it. I hope I've opened a door for you—and I know you're ready to walk through it too.

Go! Make boss moves, get unstuck, be unstoppable, and share your journey with me and others.

ABOUT THE AUTHOR

Jeannine K. Brown is the founder and managing director of Everyday Lead, an Atlanta-based national talent development and diversity consultancy firm. She leads a team that works closely with clients, delivering solutions to assist corporations in increasing retention, decreasing attrition cost, attracting new talent, and creating competitive advantages through the power of inclusion.

Since 2011, Jeannine has provided executive coaching and career strategy services to senior-level professionals and executives in many professions, including accounting and finance, entertainment, higher education, law, healthcare, pharmaceuticals, sports, technology, and more. As a highly sought-after, fun, and dynamic thought leader, Jeannine advocates for advancing women and Black professionals into fulfilling careers and executive leadership roles. She uses her active role and voice to champion the importance of diversity, equity, belonging, and inclusion among individuals, cultures, and systems.

Jeannine is the author of *Ignite! Your Best Year Ever: Achieve More and Exceed Your Potential,* published in 2016. She was named a "female success factor" in *Rolling Out* magazine for her work in diversity and inclusion, and she has been the featured cover story for *VoyageATL* and *"BMWOC (Business Men and Women of Color) Magazine."* She is a contributing thought leader and content designer for Leadercast and the Business Leadership Institute (BLI), and she can also be seen on Showtime's political docuseries, *The Circus,* season 2.

Jeannine attended the Institute of Professional Excellence in Coaching (IPEC). She is active in many professional associations and on boards of directors, including the National Association of Black Accountants Inc. and the Alabama State University Foundation Board of Directors. She has a bachelor of science in accounting from Alabama State University and a master of business administration from Robinson College, Georgia State University. She loves live musical performances and is often found listening to music, singing, and dancing.

Made in the USA
Columbia, SC
21 January 2022

54593419R00072